THE SUFFERING LETTERS
OF C H SPURGEON

THE
SUFFERING
LETTERS

of
C H Spurgeon

Annotations by
Hannah Wyncoll

With 16 colour pages of pictures of original letters

Wakeman Trust, London

THE SUFFERING LETTERS
With Annotations © Wakeman Trust 2007

THE WAKEMAN TRUST
(Wakeman Trust is a UK Registered Charity)

UK Registered Office
38 Walcot Square
London SE11 4TZ

USA Office
300 Artino Drive
Oberlin, OH 44074-1263

Website: www.wakemantrust.org

ISBN 978 1 870855 60 0

Cover design by Andrew Owen

Printed by Stephens & George, Merthyr Tydfil, UK

Contents

People said to me years ago, 'You will break your constitution down with preaching ten times a week,' and the like.

Well, if I have done so, I am glad of it. I would do the same again. If I had fifty constitutions I would rejoice to break them down in the service of the Lord Jesus Christ.

You young men that are strong, overcome the wicked one and fight for the Lord while you can. You will never regret having done all that lies in you for our blessed Lord and Master.

CHS, 1876

C. H. Spurgeon
The 'prince of preachers'
1834-1892
Pastor of the Metropolitan Tabernacle, London

Introduction

THE LETTERS in this book were written by C. H. Spurgeon during times of great illness, many not having been published before. All but a few are held by the Metropolitan Tabernacle. Mrs Susannah Spurgeon referred in her husband's auto-biography to this collection of letters as follows:

> 'Amongst the choicest of them were those addressed to the officers and members of the church at the Tabernacle, his later epistles to the beloved brethren and sisters committed to his charge. In writing to them, he often seemed to pour out his very soul in his pleading with them to be consistent, prayerful, Christian men and women, earnestly labouring for the good of the people of God amongst whom their lot was cast.'

For thirteen years up to 1867 C. H. Spurgeon was able to exert himself fully in all the many ministries built up under the auspices of the Tabernacle. But in October of that year he suffered his first serious episode of illness, and for the next 24 years sustained regular bouts of vomiting, fever and considerable pain, with swelling and rheumatic pain in his limbs, and also extreme mental exhaustion.

His work output in the light of such ill health was truly amazing.

It was thought that he suffered from rheumatic gout (following his grandfather), although Spurgeon himself said more than once that 'we call the evil gout for want of a better word, but it differs widely from the disorder which goes under that name.' Near the end of his life, his condition was diagnosed as Bright's Disease, or chronic nephritis, a disease of the kidneys, causing severe pain and swelling due to accumulation of fluid which can distend the whole body, and severely restrict breathing.

He was able to call on assistance for departments of the work from his assistant pastors and elders. His brother James served from 1868 as co-pastor, helping greatly with the running of the institutions, and he had secretarial support, especially from the 'armour-bearer' Joseph Harrald.

During times of illness Spurgeon was reassured to know the work was taken care of by those who shared his convictions and zeal, and who had great personal love towards him. Despite all this, much of the weight and responsibility of the work still lay on his shoulders, and he once spoke of having created a giant machine which would yet grind him up. However, he was always convinced that the church should be constantly pressing forward and finding new avenues of service to bring glory to the Lord and to further the gospel. His ministry was one of constant growth and increase.

The work at the Tabernacle was vast. Spurgeon often preached ten times a week both at the Tabernacle and at other meetings. The Sunday School met in the afternoon, attended by a thousand and more children, taught by over a hundred of the church members. Spurgeon encouraged and organised his people in many evangelistic activities on Sunday afternoons and evenings, especially in outreach work among the poor. On Sunday evenings in 1884 there were at least a thousand Tabernacle members going out to take meetings in various places. From the 1870s, every three months Spurgeon would ask all the members to stay away from the Sunday evening service so that there would be room for unconverted people to hear the gospel and the place would be filled. Large numbers of the Tabernacle congregation, who hardly ever left the area of south London, were involved in numerous outreach activities throughout the week.

The church had many institutions which needed constant input from Spurgeon, such as the Pastors' College, the Almshouses, the Orphanage, the Colportage Association and many evangelistic and compassionate societies, the latter usually being chaired by the elders. There were 66 of these by the time Spurgeon had been pastor for 25 years. The Pastors' College generated a great deal of work, not only in the regular interviewing, lecturing and oversight, but also in the endeavours and cares of the churches founded by former students. These founded over 200 churches in London and the home counties alone, along with some 40 missions. Men from the College were also supported as part of the Tabernacle's missionary work in Africa, China, India and other places.

Spurgeon's literary work was immense. He compiled more than 140 books, maintained the monthly *The Sword and the Trowel* magazine (from 1865), and edited the weekly sermon *(The Metropolitan Tabernacle Pulpit)* which enjoyed a considerable distribution. Amazingly, he responded to an average of 500 letters each week.

Spurgeon sometimes tried to keep Wednesdays clear of appointments and meetings as his pastor's Sabbath but rarely succeeded. At one point he wrote:

> 'No one living knows the toil and care I have to bear…I have to look after the Orphanage, have charge of a church with four thousand members, sometimes there are marriages and burials to be undertaken, there is the weekly sermon to be revised, *The Sword and the Trowel* to be edited, and besides all that, a weekly average of five hundred letters to be answered. This, however, is only half my duty, for there are innumerable churches established by friends, with the affairs of which I am closely connected, to say nothing of the cases of difficulty which are constantly being referred to me.'

Spurgeon started visiting the south of France from 1871 for a few weeks during the winter to alleviate the pain of his condition.[1] Once there, however, he did not stop his work. He would conduct morning prayers, sometimes with up to 60 people attending. He continued to edit the weekly sermon and *The Sword and the Trowel* magazine as well as continuing to work on many books, such as the seven-volume set (originally) *The Treasury of David*. He also preached, when well enough, at local churches.

The letters in this book show the great love between the pastor and his congregation, his strong and constant desire to be among them, and his concern for the Tabernacle's ministries. They certainly show the many strong encouragements to his people, revealing the exhortations to zealous activity, and providing classic quotes such as – 'Maintain the prayer meetings at blood-heat.' They provide a unique insight into the fervent activity that was, alongside the preaching, a leading feature of an historic Calvinistic church.

Before the letters, however, we provide a message given by Spurgeon on the reasons and purposes behind sickness among the Lord's people, especially his messengers.

The short sermons and editorials of Spurgeon included in this book are abridged and edited, but the letters are presented in original form.

H.W.

---

1   The first 'suffering letter' from 1871 is given in the appendix on page 154

Laid Aside – Why?
by C H Spurgeon

From *The Sword and the Trowel*, May 1876 (edited)

MYSTERIOUS are the visitations of sickness. When the Lord is using a man for his glory it is remarkable that he should suddenly smite him down and suspend his usefulness. It must be right, but the reason for it does not lie near the surface.

The sinner whose every act pollutes the society in which he moves is frequently permitted year after year to spend unabating vigour infecting all who approach him. No sickness removes him even for an hour from his deadly ministry. He is always at his post, energetic in his mission of destruction.

How is it that a heart eager for the welfare of men and the glory of God should find itself hampered by a sickly frame, and limited from its best usefulness by attacks of painful disease? We may ask the question (as long as we do so without murmuring), but who shall answer it for us?

When the advance of a body of soldiers is stopped by a volley of fire which scatters painful wounds on all sides, we understand that this is but one of the natural incidents of war; but if a commander should stop his own troops in mid-battle and proceed with his own hand to render some of his most zealous warriors incapable of service, would we not be at a loss to conceive his motives? Happily for us our happiness does not depend upon our understanding the providence of God. We are able to believe where we are not able to explain, and we are content to leave a thousand mysteries unsolved rather than tolerate a single doubt as to the wisdom and goodness of our heavenly Father. The painful malady which puts the Christian minister *hors de combat* when he is most needed in the conflict is a kind messenger from the God of love, and is to be entertained as such. We know this is the case, but exactly how it can be so we cannot tell.

Let us consider awhile. Is it not good for us to be nonplussed, puzzled, and forced to exercise our faith? Would it be good for us to have all things so ordered by God that we could see the reason for his every arrangement? Could the scheme of divine love be so supremely, infinitely, wise if we could measure it with our limited powers of reasoning? And would we not be as foolish and conceited as spoiled and over-petted children, if all things were arranged according to our judgement of what would be right and proper?

Ah, it is good to be thrown out of our depth and made to swim in the sweet waters of mighty love! We know that it is supremely blessed to be compelled to cease from self, to surrender both desire and judgement, and to lie passive in the hands of God.

It is of the utmost importance to us to be kept humble. Self-consciousness and self-importance make a hateful delusion, but one into which we fall as naturally as weeds grow on a dunghill. We cannot be used of the Lord but that we also dream of personal greatness. We think ourselves almost indispensable to the church; pillars of the cause, and foundations of the temple of God!

We are nothings and nobodies, but that we think otherwise is very evident, for as soon as we are put on the shelf we begin anxiously to enquire, 'How will the work go on without me?' The fly on the coach wheel may just as well enquire, 'How will the mails be carried without me?'

Far better men have been laid in the grave without the Lord's work having been brought to a standstill, and shall we fume and fret because for a short season we must lie upon the bed of languishing? If we were laid aside only when it was obvious that our services could be spared, then there would be no jolt to our pride, but to weaken our strength at the precise moment when our presence seems most needed is the surest way to teach us that we are not essential to God's work, and that even when we are most needed he can easily do without us. If this be the practical lesson, the rough schooling may be easily endured, for surely it is desirable beyond all things that self should be kept low and the Lord alone magnified.

In addition, may not our gracious Lord design for us a double honour when he sends a double set of trials? Abundant in labours is a high degree, but patient in suffering is in no way inferior. Some believers have excelled in active service, but have scarcely been tried in this other, equally honourable field of submissive endurance. Though veterans in work, they are little better than raw recruits in the practice of patience, and on this account they are in some respects only half developed in their Christian adulthood. May not the Lord have choice designs for some of his servants, and intend to perfect them in both forms of Christlikeness?

There seems to be no natural reason why both a person's hands should not be equally useful, but few actually become ambidextrous, because the 'left' hand is not sufficiently exercised. The left-handed men of the Scriptures were really men who had two right hands, being able to use both members with equal dexterity. Patience is the left hand of faith, and if the Lord requires an Ehud to smite Eglon, or a Benjamite to sling stones at a hair's breadth and not miss, it may be he will exercise his patience as well as his industry. Should this be so, would we wish to avoid the divine favour? Far wiser would it be to remember that such double warfare will require double grace, and involve corresponding responsibility.

A change in the mode of our personal spiritual devotions may also be highly beneficial, delivering us from unknown but serious evils. The cumbering brought about by much service, like a growth upon the bark of a fruit tree, might become injurious, and therefore our Father the husbandman with the rough instruments of pain scrapes away the obnoxious parasite.

Great walkers have assured us that they tire soonest upon level ground, but that in scaling the mountains and descending the valleys fresh muscles are brought into play, and the changed nature of the exertion together with the change of scene enables them to hold on with less fatigue. Pilgrims to Heaven can probably confirm this witness.

The continuous exercise of a single virtue demanded by particular circumstances, is exceedingly commendable, but if other graces are allowed to lie dormant the soul may become warped; and the good may be exaggerated till it is tinged with evil. Holy activities may be the means of refining a large part of our nature, but there are other equally precious areas of our born-again nature which are unaltered by them.

The early and the latter rain may be all that is required for the wheat, barley and flax, but the trees which yield the fragrant gums of Araby must first weep with the night dews. The traveller on dry land sees the handiwork of God on all sides and is filled with holy admiration, but he has not completed his education till he has tried the other element, for – 'They that go down to the sea in ships, that do business in great waters; these see the works of the Lord, and his wonders in the deep.'

It is good for a man to bear the yoke of service, and he is no loser when it is exchanged for the yoke of suffering. May not severe discipline fall to the lot of some to qualify them for their office of under-shepherds? How can we speak with consoling authority to a situation which we have never known? The complete pastor's life will be an epitome of the lives of his people, and they will turn to his preaching as men do to David's psalms, to see themselves and their sorrows, as in a mirror. Their needs will be the reason for his griefs.

As in the case of the Lord himself, perfect equipment for his work came only through suffering, and so must it be for those who are called to follow him in binding up the broken-hearted, and loosing the prisoners.

Souls still remain in our churches to whose deep and dark experiences we shall never be able to minister till we also have been plunged in the abyss where all Jehovah's waves roll over our heads. If this be the fact – and we are sure it is – then may we heartily welcome anything which will make us fitter channels of blessing. For the elect's sake it shall be joy to endure all things, and to bear a part of – 'that which is behind of the afflictions of Christ in my flesh for his body's sake, which is the church'.

It may be, alas, that there are different and far more humiliating causes for our bodily afflictions! The Lord may see in us that which grieves him and provokes him to use the rod. 'Show me wherefore thou contendest with me', should be the prompt petition of the believer's heart. 'Is there not a cause?'

It can never be superfluous to humble ourselves and institute self-examination, for even if we walk in our integrity and can lift up our face without shame in this matter concerning great sin, yet our shortcomings and omissions must cause us to blush. How much holier we ought to have been, and might have been! How much more prevalently we might have prayed! With how much more unction we might have preached! Here is endless room for tender confession before the Lord.

Yet it is not good to attribute each sickness and trial to some actual fault, as though we were under the law, or could be punished again for those sins which Jesus bore in his own body on the tree.

It would be ungenerous to others if we looked upon the greatest sufferer as necessarily the greatest sinner. Everyone knows that it would be unjust so to judge our fellow-Christians, and therefore we shall be very unwise if we apply so erroneous a rule to ourselves and morbidly condemn ourselves when God condemns not.

Just now, when anguish fills the heart, and the spirits are bruised with sore pain and travail, it is not the best time for forming a candid judgement of our own condition, or of anything else. Let the judging faculty yield to good sense, and let us with tears of loving confession throw ourselves upon our Father's bosom, and looking up into his face believe that he loves us with all his infinite heart. 'Though he slay me, yet will I trust in him,' shall be our one unvarying determination, and may the eternal Spirit work in us a perfect acquiescence in the whole will of God, whatever that may be.

PART 1
1876-83

In 1871, for the first time, Spurgeon was advised to rest overseas where the weather was thought to be curative to his condition, and pressures of work would not be so immediately upon him. He travelled to Italy in November 1871. (The very first 'home-letter', written from Rome, is in the Appendix.) During this first journey time was spent at Menton on the south coast of France, where Spurgeon subsequently went almost every winter until his death.

His publisher Joseph Passmore, among others, was with him on the first trip, and in future years he was almost always one of the group accompanying Spurgeon. Joseph Harrald, Spurgeon's secretary, usually went with him from 1879.

During the time that this first group of letters were written (some from his home in London but most from the continent), Spurgeon endured many bouts of severe illness, but also, happily, stretches of busy and fruitful labour. The membership of the Tabernacle by this time exceeded 5,000 and activity in all the areas of ministry proceeded apace.

By the end of this phase of his ministry the Spurgeon household had moved to 'Westwood', Upper Norwood, in the hope that the higher ground would prevent him having to go away each winter, but the health benefit was not as great as anticipated.

Nightingale Lane
Clapham
23rd April 1876

Beloved Friends,

After ten days of very great pain I am now improving but I am not yet able to walk across my room. I am sure this is right, for the Lord has done it.

My great trouble is that I cannot preach and go on with the Master's work, but in answer to your prayers I believe I shall soon be restored.

I am a poor weak creature to be Pastor of such a church but I feel sure that your great love will have patience with me. Every atom of strength I am delighted to use in your service but the burden is heavy and my mind occasionally wearies under it. Then the flesh sympathises and I become a prisoner, laid by the heels.

I hope the inability of the Pastor will be a call to every member of the church to do all within his or her power to win souls and build up the church. Let everything go on better than if I were among you: above all, I beseech you pray more. A special prayer meeting would do more to make me well than all the drugs in Apothecaries Hall, good as they may be.

I long to see hundreds saved and added to the church. Are there not some in the congregation who will today decide to be on the Lord's side?

Yours in deep love
C. H. Spurgeon

(Portion of original)

Nightingale Lane
Clapham
30th April 1876

Beloved Friends,

Up till yesterday I had indulged the pleasant hope of preaching this morning, but on Friday night I had a fresh attack of severe pain and I have not since been able to leave my bed. I hope you will have patience with your poor sick Pastor who is anxious to be at his work but is quite unable to stand, and not very able to think.

Although great pain often disturbs the judgement I thank God I have not been allowed to doubt the goodness of the Lord in afflicting me, I bless his holy name for every sharp pang, and I entreat him to bring forth some good thing out of this present evil. If he will but glorify himself in me or by me I shall be the happiest of men.

Dear Christian brethren, work for Jesus while you can, for you too may be laid aside.

Unconverted ones, seek the Lord at once, for you may soon be gone beyond the reach of mercy.

Pray that the two beloved brethren, who have so kindly undertaken my work today, may have great success in their preaching. They have put themselves to great inconvenience to come and therefore deserve our loving gratitude.

Do pray for me. I suffer much and am sometimes very low. Yet I know the Lord is good.

Yours very lovingly
C. H. Spurgeon

(Portion of original)

Unconverted ones, seek the Lord at once, for you may soon be gone beyond the reach of mercy

Nightingale Lane
Clapham
7th May 1876

Beloved Friends,

I feel very low, weak, and full of pain this morning and cannot write much. I try to be patient but I pant to be with you, engaged in my loved work again. Pray for me I entreat you, and then I shall hope to be at my post next Lord's Day.

The arrangement for next Sunday as to admission must now be given up: your tickets will be available and I trust all of you will be in your places. Another quarter, if the Lord will, we shall hope to carry out the proposed plan. I am much grieved to have to give it up on this occasion.

Your great love and patience are much comfort to me. I pray believers to do more for Jesus to make up for my absence, and I beseech the Lord to save those who are still undecided, and bless the ministry of those who occupy my place. I suffer greatly just now: if the Lord will work among you in my absence I shall be consoled indeed. O live for eternity and work for Jesus while you can.

Your suffering minister

C. H. Spurgeon

The proposed plan mentioned here was carried out on 16th July 1876. On the Lord's Day evening service the members and seat-holders at the Tabernacle were asked to stay away, leaving the building free for strangers. Spurgeon recorded that, 'Crowds of strangers poured in, the richest and the poorest being alike represented, until the Tabernacle was full as a barrel packed with herrings…Our own beloved people held three prayer meetings, and an open air service while we were preaching, and so lost nothing themselves.' This plan was subsequently repeated every three months.

Cannes
31st January [probably 1878]

To my beloved Church and Congregation,
Dear Friends,

The journey here is long for one who is in weak health, and I have had but a few days of rest, but already I feel myself improving. The Master's service among you has been very delightful to me; but it has grown to such proportions that I have felt the burden of it upon my spirits, and I have suffered more depression of heart, and weariness of mind than I could well express. Rest I could not find at home, where every hour has its cares; but here I cease altogether from these things and the mind becomes like an unstrung bow, and so regains its elasticity.

I wish I could work on among you continually and never even pause, but many infirmities show that this cannot be. Pray therefore that this needful break in my work may strengthen me for a long spring and summer campaign.

Nothing can so cheer me as to know that all of you are living for Jesus and living like him. Our church has produced great workers in the past and I hope the sacred enthusiasm which they manifested will never burn low among us. Jesus is worth being served with our best, yea with our all, and that in an intense and all-consuming manner. May our young men and women love the Lord much and win others to him by their zeal for God, and may our elder brethren and the matrons among us prove ever the pillars of the church in their holy conversation and devout godliness.

Maintain the prayer meetings at blood-heat. See well to the schools and all the classes, and other labours for Jesus Christ. Let nothing flag of prayer, service, or offering. We have a great trust, may the ➤

➢ Lord make us faithful to it.

My love is with you all and my prayers for your welfare.

O that you who are still unsaved may be led to Jesus through those who supply my lack of service. Peace with the co-pastor, deacons and elders and with you all. From your loving but unworthy Pastor

C. H. Spurgeon

(Portion of original)

Menton
28th February 1878

Beloved Friends,

I rejoice that the time of my return to you is now a matter of a few days and that I have every prospect, if the Lord will, of returning with health established and mind restored. Perhaps never before have I been brought so low in spirit, and assuredly never more graciously restored. May the Lord sanctify both the trial and the recovery, so that I may be a fitter instrument in his hand to promote his glory and your highest good.

The last fortnight of additional rest was wisely ordained by a higher hand than that of the good deacons who suggested it to me, for without it I should not have had space to pass through an attack of pain which had just swept over me, and left me improved by its violence. The last few days will, I feel, be the best of the whole, when I shall not have to be thoughtful of recovery but altogether restful.

Good news from Tabernacle continues to be as cold waters to a thirsty soul. You have had great times of refreshing; may their influence abide with you. We must not go to sleep on my return nor at any other time, but steadily labour on and watch for souls. Spurts are very helpful, but to keep up the pace at a high regular figure is the most important thing. Even an invalid can make a great exertion when some remarkable occasion excites him to do so, but constant unwearied effort belongs only to those who have stamina and inward ➤

> Spurgeon was back in the Tabernacle pulpit on 17th March, and until November was in much better health and busy in all areas of the work.
> He was full of joy that year to see the 'first fruits' of the orphanage work as an 'old boy' took up a pastorate in Cambridgeshire. The membership roll of the Tabernacle that year was over 5,000 despite a 'battalion' of 250 being sent to form a new church in Peckham. There were now 100 students in the Pastors' College.

➤ force. May our whole church prove itself to be strong in the Lord and in the power of his might by increasingly carrying on its work of faith and labour of love.

In these days we are regarded as Puritanical and old-fashioned, and this, I trust, we shall never be ashamed of, but wear it as an ornament. The old orthodox faith is to us no outworn creed of past ages but a thing of power, a joy for ever. In the name of the Lord who by that faith is honoured we press forward to proclaim again and again the doctrines of the grace of God, the efficacy of the blood of the Divine Substitute, and the power of the Eternal Spirit; and we feel assured that whoever may oppose, the omnipotent gospel will prevail. The multitudes are hungering for that old-fashioned bread whereon their fathers fed, and too many preachers now give them newly carved stones, and bid them admire the skill of the modern sculptors. We mean to keep to the distribution of bread and the stone-cutters will meet with no competition from us in their favourite amusement. But, brethren, only a living church, holy, prayerful, active – can make the old truth victorious. Linked with a mass of mere profession it will perform no exploits. To you and to me there is a growing call for greater spirituality and more divine power, for the work before us increases in difficulty.

The Lord be with you all, and with your pastor, deacons and elders.

So prays your loving

C. H. Spurgeon

In these days we are regarded as Puritanical a-old-fashioned, &this, I trust, we shall never be ashamed of

(Portion of original)

Nightingale Lane, Balham, Surrey
[Shortly before Spurgeon left for Menton on 15th January 1879]

Beloved Friends,

You will be glad to know that I am certainly better, and have only now to rise above the extreme weakness left by pain. The deacons and elders have unanimously requested me to take three months rest, and as I believe that they well represent the church, and as moreover I see the necessity for following their kind advice, I shall, if the Lord will, do as they prescribe. I earnestly pray that during my absence no interest may suffer and no holy work may flag. I would gladly stand at my post, but I cannot, therefore all I can do is to offer prayer for those who will occupy my place that they may feed you with knowledge and understanding and that your souls may be full of life and activity before the Lord.

I again thank from my inmost heart those who have by their generosity and diligence made 'the Testimonial' to be so wonderful a success. It overcomes one to think how well, how earnestly, how happily all was done. But now for a spiritual blessing, which shall be still more wonderful. It is even more to be desired, let it be sought and laboured for. The February meetings if followed up with universal zeal, will by the blessing of our God, bring us a great revival, and a large increase. O that it might come.

I shall be far away but my heart is with you always. Peace be to the whole beloved church and joy in the Lord.

Your afflicted Pastor

C. H. Spurgeon

> The Testimonial referred to here was to mark Spurgeon's 'silver wedding' after twenty-five years as Pastor. Over £6,000 was raised as a gift to him, £5,000 of which he gave to the Almshouses and the rest to the other institutions. He was also presented with a clock for his study.

Appended to the weekly printed sermon.

Menton

January 1879

Dear Friends,

The sermon is so long that only a line or so is left for me. I will say the less of myself. The warm sunny days which I have spent in this retreat are, by God's blessing, bringing back to me health and strength. I shall be happy indeed if my mental and spiritual vigour should also be renewed by the removal of the daily care which pressed upon me; if it be so my hearers shall be the gainers, for all my strength has been and ever shall be laid out in my ministry.

I am right glad to hear that special services are commencing at the Tabernacle, and I entreat all the brethren there to throw all their energies into them. Pray that the Holy Spirit may work mightily and glorify the Lord Jesus in the midst of the congregations; and then set to work to fetch in the people from the outside. Gather them! Gather them from hedge and highway, and crowd the gospel feast. The preachers are among you whom God has widely blest, but how can they benefit the people if they do not come to hear them? Make the services known and press those to come who do not usually attend public worship. We long to see souls saved, – do we not? My heart cannot be content while men are being lost. I cannot be among the crowds to preach, but my inmost soul prays for those who are indulged with that privilege, and for you also who have the joy of helping on the work of the Lord.

I am bound to thank those generous friends who continue to send aid to the various works under my care: the Lord reward them. To each and all my hearers and readers I send my hearty Christian salutations.

C. H. Spurgeon

Menton
6th February 1879

To my Church and people

Dear Friends,

I am hoping and praying that the special services at the Tabernacle may excel all that have gone before.

To urge you to the utmost earnestness about these I have written the short sermon which will be published this week. It would give me great joy to hear, as I feel sure I shall, that in this as in all the other works of the church you are abundantly filled with zeal and constancy.

> Three short sermons written by Spurgeon during this stay in Menton are provided starting on page 135.

My one concern is lest the Lord's work should suffer by my absence: I entreat you do not permit it to be so in any one point or degree.

The damp and dull weather which has reached us even here has somewhat retarded my progress to health and strength so that I remain a very feeble traveller; but yet I am greatly improved and feel that my mind and spirits are the better for the rest.

To all of you from the bottom of my heart I send my sincere love in Christ Jesus.

Yours to serve while there remains any life in me
C. H. Spurgeon

(Portion of original)

Appended to the weekly printed sermon.

Menton
20th February 1879

Beloved Friends,

By the time that this note is printed the special services at the Tabernacle will be drawing to a close, and it will be meet to harrow in the seed with renewed supplication. Shall so much effort be in vain? It cannot be; and yet everything depends upon the mighty working of the Spirit of God, and therefore we must seek his face if we would see large results. I suggest that every sermon reader should spend a special time in prayer next Sabbath-day in pleading for the revival of evangelical religion. *The Times* pronounced the funeral oration of the evangelical party, but it is not even dead within the Established Church, and certainly not among Dissenters. Let us, however, pray that it may exhibit more vigorous life. There is need of such supplication, but it must be presented in faith and with holy importunity. So let it be.

For myself, one word only. I am recovering, and rest is restoring mind and heart. Pray for me.

Yours to serve always

C. H. Spurgeon

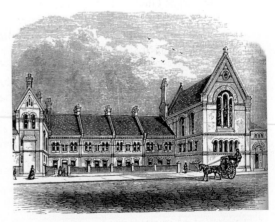

The Tabernacle Almshouses, Walworth. These had been started by Dr John Rippon to house and care for needy widows. Spurgeon rebuilt the Almshouses nearer to the Tabernacle.

Menton

5th March 1879

With great gratitude to God I am able to report myself as restored to health and spirits. I am still very far from strong upon my feet, and after a short walk I suffer pain in the knees; but even this is improving and I have every reason to hope and believe that at the appointed time I shall be fully able to resume my beloved labour. I desire to present loving salutations to all the beloved members of my church, and to wish them each one every blessing.

C. H. Spurgeon

Spurgeon returned to London in April very much improved in health. The Easter Sunday service was one of thanksgiving taken from *Psalm 145.7*, 'They shall abundantly utter the memory of thy great goodness.'

The following months were filled with numerous meetings, also the annual College Conference, and literary labours.

May saw the special meeting to mark 25 years as Pastor. Spurgeon explained why he gave the whole of the Testimonial Fund to the Lord's work in these words: 'When I gave myself up to him at first to be his minister I never reckoned that he would give anything except raiment to put on and bread to eat. I recollect when my income was forty-five pounds a year. Well, I do not know, but I think I had more money to spare then than I have got now. I had not many things to drag at me then; I never wanted anything. When I came to London I desired to keep up the feeling that I was to serve God altogether, and give myself and all that I should ever get entirely to him, and just be a gentleman-commoner upon the bounty of God…I get sometimes requests for loans of hundreds of pounds, under the supposition that I am a very rich man. I never was a rich man, and never shall be; and yet I am the richest man in England, if you can make that out, because there is nothing that I want on earth but I have it. I have not any wishes which are not gratified and satisfied, except that I always want to be doing more for Jesus Christ, if possible.'

Appended to the weekly printed sermon.

Hotel de la Paix, Menton
14th November 1879

To my Church, Congregation, and Sermon Readers
Dear Friends,

During my absence you expect to hear from me by means of a little note at the end of the weekly sermon. The kindly interest which suggests this expectation is very precious to me, and therefore I will not disappoint it. I would run the risk of being egotistical rather than treat Christian affection with coolness. There is none too much of it in the world, and where it survives it deserves to be cultivated. More than most men I am favoured with brotherly love, and I am most grateful for it.

I have commenced a short period of rest in this delightful region. Taking the advice of physicians, I left before rheumatic affections had prostrated me, and I am in hope that I shall in this genial climate escape my usual attack, and gather strength, and then return in the middle of January fortified to endure the rest of the winter. On former occasions the major part of my vacation has been spent in slowly recovering from weakness of body and depression of spirit, but this time I trust it will be used in gathering thoughts and storing force for future use. Pray for me that it may be so, for I would fain carry on the work of the Lord without the serious hindrances caused by the sicknesses of former years.

Dear friends at home, I entreat you suffer nothing to decline. Cheer by your presence those who preach for me. Keep up the prayer meetings and the week-night services, and sustain the offering for the College, which is at present somewhat behind. It will need more than £40 each week to make up the £1,879.

The weekly sermon is always carefully prepared by me, and it will not be less interesting because it does not happen to have been preached last Sunday. The discourse will be as new to most of my readers as if it were delivered yesterday, since they have never seen or heard it before. I hope to write a few sermonettes under the olive trees, and I will do my very best to make them interesting. I pray my readers, therefore, not to imagine that my absence from London will make any difference to the weekly publication of these sermons. I hope that a little thoughtful repose will enable me to preach better when I return, but otherwise my temporary absence from England will not affect the regular weekly issue of the *Tabernacle Pulpit*.

A month or so ago the sermon entitled 'Among the Lions' excited unusual interest. I hope that the present sermon, entitled 'The Dromedaries', will be found equally useful, though it is not a solace for the slandered, but a stimulus for the active.

With fervent Christian affection,

Yours most heartily

C. H. Spurgeon

Spurgeon's view of slavery

Spurgeon was very firm in his view of slavery and although he knew it would cause a decrease in financial support he made clear statements on this. In America his income from publications was indeed diminished and in some places in the southern states effigies of Spurgeon were burned, although this feeling against him did not last as the years passed.

'I do from my inmost soul detest slavery…and although I commune at the Lord's Table with men of all creeds, yet with a slave-holder I have no fellowship of any sort or kind. Whenever one has called upon me, I have considered it my duty to express my detestation of his wickedness, and I would as soon think of receiving a murderer into my church…as a man-stealer.'

Hotel de la Paix, Menton
24th November 1879

To Deacons and Elders

Dear Friends,

After the first week I was overtaken by that insidious rheumatic affection which seems to be in my constitution, and I have now been ill these nine days, with the right foot first and then with the left hand. It was a source of great thankfulness to me that the attack, painful as it was, came upon me when I was not required to be in the pulpit, or engaged in my Lord's work: and again it was comfortable to be in a warm and dry climate where everything is in my favour. By God's goodness I am carefully attended by one of the most skilful of physicians, who has for some years been my friend, namely Dr Bennet, and by the divine blessing I hope soon to recover. I can already walk, and if it were not that my hand is quite useless and the whole arm very uneasy, I should be able to speak of the attack as over.

I write not only to send my love to all my beloved friends at Tabernacle, but also to mention my concern for the poor people who have suffered by the inundations around you.

I hope the Tabernacle will not be behind in doing something to help. I leave it to the discretion of the officers to say what shall be done. I will cheerfully contribute £50 myself, if there appears to be a lack of funds. A committee should be formed to attend first to our own poor brethren, and then to all others who may need. In any case it would be grievous to my feelings to be out of the way when need is

Spurgeon returned to Menton in November.

The flooding referred to in this letter was the result of an appallingly wet summer. Cold, wet weather also delayed the ripening of the harvest, so that even in East Anglia some crops had not been gathered in by Christmas, contributing to a serious depression for British agriculture.

While Spurgeon was away, Mrs Hillyard, the founding sponsor of the Orphanage, died. Her last words were, 'My boys! my boys!'

around us, and as I am so in person, I write to show that I am not in spirit. Act then at once.

I earnestly trust that the brethren who have served you in my absence have been acceptable to saints, and have been the means of the conversion of sinners, and that the special services have had rich results.

I mention no one's name in this brief note, but I send my love to all my dearly beloved helpers, deacons and elders, and members; never more dear than now.

You do pray for me. The Lord bless you all as only he can.

Your right hearty friend and loving Pastor

C. H. Spurgeon

Spurgeon and his private secretary Joseph W. Harrald in the study at Westwood

Hotel de la Paix, Menton
4th December 1879

Appended to the weekly printed sermon.

Dear Friends,

I had hoped to have prepared a new sermon for you this week, but instead thereof I have been altogether laid aside, and quite unable either to use brain to think or hand to write with. It must be right that I should thus be periodically rendered useless, but I wish I were fit to be trusted with the privilege of constant activity. Some tools are not well enough constructed to be kept in constant use; much of their time must be spent in being repaired. Please pray for me that in my case the reparations may be well done, and that I may be strengthened to accomplish better and greater service for my Master than ever before.

This week's sermon is one touching the matter nearest my heart. Oh that it may be read with such practical attention as to lead to its being carried out! Soul winners are the great need of the times. We all do enough of talking and scheming, but living in the life of God and going forth in the divine power derived therefrom to pluck sinners from the burning are far too rare.

Receive, dear friends, the warmest affection of

Your greatly suffering Pastor

C. H. Spurgeon

The sermon referred to in this letter, 'Soul Saving Our One Great Business', derives from *1 Corinthians 9.22* – Paul's reasons for making evangelism the highest priority in his ministry.

'I ask every worker here to see to this, that he never turns aside from shooting at this target, and at the very centre of this target too, namely, that he may win souls for Christ, and see them born to God, and washed in the fountain filled with blood. Let the workers' hearts ache, and yearn, and their voices cry until their throats are hoarse, but let them judge that they have accomplished nothing whatever until at least, in some cases, men are really saved.'

(*Metropolitan Tabernacle Pulpit* No. 1507, 1879)

Menton
28th December 1879

My beloved Friends,

Now that our special services are beginning I entreat you to labour as one man to
make them a success. It is the Lord's work
to send the blessing, but as a rule he begins
to work upon sinners by first of all arousing
his own people. We believe in grace, and in
grace alone, but we know by experience that
true revival is not a gourd which springs
up on a sudden while men sleep, but like the angel of Bethlehem it
visits those who keep watch over their flocks by night. Grace to us is
as new wine, refreshing and inspiring, and not as a soporific potion
creating the slumber of inaction. Messrs Smith and Fullerton, who
conduct the services, have proved their fitness for the position by
their success in other congregations. If the pleasure of the Lord does
not prosper in their hand among us, it will be our fault, and not
theirs.

What is wanted is, first, much prayer. In this, all the Lord's people
can join. Attend the noon prayer meeting, if possible, and if not, pray
all the same. Without the Holy Spirit we are nothing, and prayer
alone can win his aid. The next practical step is to make the meetings
known. The people cannot come to the services if they do not know
of them. The expense of advertising is very great if left to be done
by the home authorities; but if every person will spread the news,
this method of gaining publicity is the most effective, and it can be
done on the largest scale with very little outlay. If you cannot preach
the gospel you may yet win a soul by letting it be known that the
gospel is preached. The third needful work is to bring in the people. ➤

Spurgeon printed this letter in *The Sword and the Trowel* in February 1880 saying – 'We insert the following letter which we sent home, because it may show to other churches how all the members can aid special services, and under the divine bless-ing secure success.'

➢ Persuade friends and neighbours to attend. Canvass a district. Visit from house to house with invitations. 'Compel them to come in,' and when this is done, give a personal word. Speak for Jesus, if it be with faltering lips, both before and after the addresses of the preachers. Good sermons need following up by personal entreaties. God often blesses feeble efforts; indeed, he suffers no true endeavour to fall to the ground. How I wish I could persuade ALL the church members to rally to the Holy War! God knoweth how much I wish I could be with you myself. My infirmities detain me from the field of sacred action, but my heart watches you. As ye have served the Lord in my presence, so do I pray you much more in my absence; that if possible my lack of service may be made up by your overplus of labour. You have not only your own work to do, but mine also. Be pastors to the lambs, and to the wandering sheep. If you cannot fill the pulpit, yet tell out the same 'old, old story' which is the one sole message with which it has for many years resounded. To your beloved deacons and elders, and to you all, I send my fervent Christian love, beseeching you all, all together, with all your strength, to unite in the service of love.

Yours most heartily
C. H. Spurgeon

Spurgeon with a group of boys at the orphanage in September 1890

Menton

7th January 1880

Dear Brethren,

Mr Stiff has just given me your loving letter. I hasten to thank you heartily. I will say no more now than this: my health is such that I will agree to take at least one week more and you had better provide for one Sabbath immediately. I would suggest Mr Wood of Holloway.

I write to save post and will write at length tomorrow. God bless you evermore.

Yours heartily

C. H. Spurgeon

1880 was another busy year with more than 450 new members. Since 1868, 511 men had been through the College, those volunteering information having baptised 39,000 people. Spurgeon said of them – 'I feel thankful that so large a proportion of the men have continued in the work, remaining unchanged in their sentiments…Of course there are failures; we cannot guarantee men. We cannot guarantee a horse, and certainly we cannot a man, for, in addition to all the infirmities of the body which an animal has, there are infirmities of mind and spirit possessed by a man, so that one who is a capital student may turn out a very poor preacher, and one who has been a first-rate student will suddenly drop and we cannot tell who. Sometimes he gets in love, which is good or bad according to whom he loves; or he gets a crotchet, rides a hobby, understands the book of *Revelation* better than he understands *Matthew, Mark* or *Romans*. Some fad takes him, or else he gets self-indulgent…But it is a blessing that this matter has been but a very small affliction with us. On the contrary we have had joy in the brethren.'

In June the memorial-stones were laid for four houses of the Girls' Orphanage. There were to be 250 girls housed in addition to the 250 boys. Spurgeon and his publishers met the cost of one of the houses and called it, 'Sermon House' because as Spurgeon said – 'the College, the Orphanage, and all our works owe a great deal to the sermons. I have a little church of some 5,500 members at Newington Butts; but I have a larger church of, I dare say, 56,000 members all over England, Scotland and Ireland, who are always up to the mark if any good work has to be done…This house is to be a record to all time of our thankfulness to God that the sermons have continued to be printed week by week for twenty-five and a half years.'

Westwood, Beulah Hill, Upper Norwood
19th September 1880

Dear Friends,

Since worshipping with you at the prayer meeting last Monday evening I have suffered greatly and have been quite laid aside. I beg your loving prayers that I may soon recover, and yet more, that I may gather blessing from the sharp affliction.

It is something to have had 6 months of uninterrupted work among you, and even this painful break will not I hope be a long one. Your great patience will bear with a poor crippled minister, and I shall not fail to attempt all that my limited power can accomplish. God will use my weakness, and his cause shall be girded with strength.

Today the collections are to meet the large extra expenses incurred by most desirable repairs. We are not accustomed to deficits at the end of the year, but there will be one unless all friends feel that they must bear a share of the burden. I will not let the idea linger on my mind, for when tossing about with pain cares are bad companions.

At the Monday prayer meeting I beg special prayer for the College and the Colportage, and for the work in general which God has committed to these feeble hands.

Am I not happy to have a son to occupy my place this day? Blessed be God for it. My deepest love is ever with my dear people, but I cannot express it, or indeed express anything, for the mind suffers with the body.

Yours ever heartily
C. H. Spurgeon

In 1866 Spurgeon formed the Metropolitan Tabernacle Colportage Association. This started with just two full-time colporteurs who were employed to go from place to place distributing tracts and sermons, selling Bibles and books, and speaking to individuals and households about the gospel. They also held services and Sunday Schools. The number of colporteurs rose rapidly eventually nearly reaching 100. Most worked in rural areas where Christian influence was hardly seen. During the 25 years up to Spurgeon's death, they recorded 11,822,637 visits to families.

Westwood, Beulah Hill, Upper Norwood
3rd October 1880

Dear Friends,

I trust the storm is now over but it leaves me weak as a bruised reed. I hope that the good Physician's hand will now speedily restore me, and give me the great joy of being once more in your midst. On former occasions I have risen almost as rapidly as I went down and I hope it will be so now. For all your loving consideration of me in my sharp affliction I thank you heartily and pray God bless you all.

I earnestly beg you to make the meetings of the Baptist Union a great success. On Monday and Thursday there ought to be enthusiastic crowds. I had engaged to speak on Monday but I deeply regret that it is impossible. It is the missionary night – make it a great one, and give a prophecy of the vigour of the rest of the week.

Spurgeon, followed by the Tabernacle, was to leave the Baptist Union in 1887, during the 'Downgrade Controversy'.

On Thursday, if I can, I will be present if only to say a few words. It is to be the closing meeting and it should be the crown of all.

Pray that God may bless these gatherings to the refreshing of his ministers, and so to the benefit of the churches. He will hear you.

In coming back into work I find many cares buzzing around me which I will drive off by crying unto God. Join me in my petitions that the work of the Lord may not flag in any respect, or know any sort of lack. I have no cares but for the ark of the Lord, and that is in safe keeping.

May the sermons of today be more useful than mine would have been, and some be brought to Jesus by them who have never come at my calling.

Yours in bonds of true Christian love
C. H. Spurgeon

Westwood, Beulah Hill, Upper Norwood
9th January 1881

My Dear Friends,

The past week has been full of disappointment and anguish. My pain came upon me in furious gusts and beat me back when I thought I was within sight of shore.

I have endured as much as I can imagine one poor body to be capable of; but, blessed be God, the fury of the storm seems this morning to have abated. Pray for me that I may be permitted speedily to recover.

Our family gathering and the visit of the deacons on our silver wedding were both postponed owing to my being so much worse. Ah me! This is trying work – this pain and down-casting. Still through your prayers it will pass away and he who is the health of my countenance and my God will yet appear to me.

The kindness of friends both at the Tabernacle and far away has been overwhelming. If I cannot tell my pain, so neither can I recount my mercies. The Lord is good and blessed be his name.

Receive my grateful love.

Yours in Christ Jesus

C. H. Spurgeon

> Having celebrated his 25th 'silver wedding' as Pastor of the Tabernacle in 1879, Charles and Susannah now celebrated their personal wedding anniversary.

An anniversary picture. Mrs Spurgeon was very ill from the age of 33. She had surgery by Sir James Simpson, but her condition was still serious and she was unable to attend services for years, serving the Lord through her Book Fund. Only on the last Menton trip in 1891-2 was Mrs Spurgeon well enough to travel.

6th November 1881

Dear Friends,

By leaving home at once I hope to escape the damps of the present season and to gather strength by which I may get through the winter without a break-down. You all know how I delight in my work, and with what reluctance I leave it even for a short time, but the dread of my painful infirmity, and the conviction that my mind needs a little repose, compel me to leave you for a brief period.

I thought you would be pleased to know how the pulpit will be supplied. My brother and well beloved co-pastor will usually preach on Thursday evenings, and I am sure those who faithfully fill up their places will find themselves gratified and edified by his able teaching. The Sunday services are planned as follows:–

Nov.	13,	Mr R. H. Lovell
	20,	Mr D. L. Moody
	27,	(morning) Mr A. G. Brown
	27,	(evening) Mr W. Y. Fullerton
Dec.	4,	(morning) Mr C. Spurgeon
	4,	(evening) Mr J. A. Spurgeon
	11,	Mr R. H. Lovell
	18,	(morning) Mr J. Jackson Wray
	18,	(evening) Mr W. Y. Fullerton

No public appeals were made by D. L. Moody on his visits to the Tabernacle. He was very reluctant to preach, being intimidated by his esteem for Spurgeon, writing, 'I should consider it an honour to black your boots; but to preach to your people would be out of the question.'

On the Sunday which is allotted to our honoured friend, Mr Moody, you may expect a vast crowd, far greater than will be accommodated, and I earnestly recommend those friends who have no sittings to take the vacant ones immediately that they may secure easy admission for themselves or their friends. If it were known by the general public that any seats could be obtained they would be ➤

➤ taken at once, but it would afford me far more pleasure to see our members and regular adherents accommodated.

Be sure to keep up all the services in full vigour during my absence, and especially the prayer meetings. Those who attend my own favourite gathering on Thursday evenings at 6 are pledged to keep it going, but I hope others will unite with them.

Mr Moody will inaugurate a series of evangelistic services, which will be continued by our beloved brethren Messrs Fullerton and Smith. They will commence on Nov 21, and continue till Dec 18: but of the services themselves further particulars will be made known when the brethren have made their arrangements. I want one and all to resolve that these services shall be a great success. You can only secure this by much prayer and personal effort, and frequent attendance. Fetch in the unconverted, plead with God for them, and tell them the gospel simply, and out of your own hearts. I hope the meetings will not require expensive advertising, but that you will do this by making them known by personal statement. On this occasion I trust that care will be taken that the work pays for itself through the offerings of those who sympathise with the effort. All other churches visited by the evangelists have of late supplied their maintenance, and those who are in our church must not fall short. We do not want the unconcerned to give, but those who profit by the word will feel it to be a pleasure to communicate of their temporal things to those who give them of their spiritual things.

In leaving the work at this time I feel much confidence in my long-tried and willing friends that they will allow nothing to droop; and I hope in the Lord also that he will not suffer his own work to lose by the weakness of his servant. The College will still need your loving help: keep up the weekly offering. The Orphanage must not be forgotten: work hard for the bazaar, in which every one of us must take a share, for the sake of our poor orphan girls.

By all the love of these seven-and-twenty years I am more than ever bound to you. Abide in happy union with each other, in holy union with Jesus. Rally around my dear brother, and your deacons and elders. Let me have joy of you more and more, and may the presence of the Lord be ever with you.

Your loving Pastor

C. H. Spurgeon

Especially let all members of the Church be up & doing; for time is short

(Portion of original)

Menton
19th November 1881

To Friends at home,

I am happily resting. Pray that I may gather strength in body, soul, and spirit, and return to my labour to perform a far greater work than has ever been given me hitherto. At this time revival services are being held at the Tabernacle and I beg all friends to strive together in their prayers for a great and extraordinary blessing. Especially let all members of the church be up and doing; for time is short, men are dying, wickedness abounds and there is need that the gospel be preached with power.

With fervent love in Christ Jesus.

Yours for ever

C. H. Spurgeon

During Spurgeon's long times of illness, the many ministries at the Tabernacle continued to be blessed. Mr Carr (deacon) wrote to him during one of his absences – 'Your long affliction, and your tedious banishment, have already borne some peaceable fruits. The stable character of your work has been proved. Had the church been built on the basis of your popularity as a preacher, the congregations would not have been so well kept up in your absence; but, so far from that being the case, the prayer meetings and the weekly communion services are well attended, even when the severe weather, had you been here, would have been sufficient to account for some deficiencies.' Spurgeon left for Menton in early November 1881, returning in time to present the Christmas festivities at the Orphanage. The Prime Minister, W. E. Gladstone, visited the Tabernacle on Sunday evening of January 8th 1882.

[Undated]

Dearly Beloved Friends,

I am right glad that those who filled my place last Sabbath were so graciously enabled to feed your souls. It matters little who distributes the bread so that it comes fresh from Jesu's hand. I join you in earnest prayer that the brethren who have so generously come to my relief this day may have equally adequate assistance from our Lord and his Spirit. I thank them, but I also envy them, and would gladly pay a king's ransom, if I had it, for the privilege of preaching this day. My envy condenses into a prayer that all my Lord's ambassadors may have good speed this day that so his kingdom of peace may mightily grow in the land.

After enduring much intense pain I am now recovering and like a little child am learning to stand, and to totter from chair to chair. The trial is hot but does not last long, and there is herein much cause for gratitude. My last two attacks have been of this character. It may be the will of God that I should have many more of these singular seizures and if so I hope you will have patience with me. I have done all as to diet, abstinence from stimulants, and so on which could be done, and as the evil still continues the cause must lie elsewhere. We call the evil gout for want of a name but it differs very much from that which goes under that name. On the two last occasions I had an unusual pressure of work upon me and I broke down. My position among you is such that I can just keep on at medium pace if I have nothing extra, but the extra labour overthrows me. If I were an iron man you should have my whole strength till the last particle had been worn away but as I am only dust you must take from me what I can render and look for no more. May that service which I can render be accepted of the Lord.

I now commend you, dear Friends, to the Lord's keeping. Nothing will cheer me so much as to hear that God is among you and this I ➤

➤ shall judge of by importunate prayer meetings, good works of the church systematically and liberally sustained, and converts coming forward to confess their faith in Christ. This last I look for and long for every week. Who is on the Lord's side? Who? Wounded on the battlefield I raise myself on my arm and cry to those around me and urge them to espouse my Master's cause, for if we were wounded or dead for his sake all would be gain. By the splendour of redeeming love I charge each believer to confess his Lord and live wholly to him.

Yours for Jesus Christ's sake

C. H. Spurgeon

Spurgeon preaching in the Tabernacle, 1891

Menton, 7th February [year not stated]

My Beloved Friends,

After enjoying a few restful nights and quiet days I feel myself coming round again, and my heart is full of praise and thanksgiving to our gracious God. Your prayers have been incessant and have prevailed and I am very grateful to you all. So long as I am able to do so it will be my joy to be of service to you, and my only grief has been that sickness weakened my powers and rendered me less able to discharge my happy duties among you. The post I occupy needs a man at his best, and I have of late been very much the reverse. However, we know who it is that giveth strength to the faint and so we trust that feeble efforts have not been ineffectual.

I shall be doubly indebted to the goodness of our Lord if the remainder of my rest shall confirm the beneficial work which has commenced. I have feared that my mind would fail me. That fear is now gone but I cannot tell how I should be if I were in the thick of work at once. The further repose will I hope make me stronger for the future.

I have not yet heard tidings of the special services, but I hope that every member is at work to make them a success. Pray about them, speak about them, attend them, assist in them, bring others to them. Our two evangelists are the right instruments, but the hand is needed to work by them. Call upon him whose hand it is, and he will work according to his own good pleasure. The times are such that churches holding the old truths had need be active and energetic that the power of the gospel may be manifest to all. We need to uplift a banner because of the truth. So numerous a church as ours may accomplish great things by the power of the Holy Ghost if only we are once in downright earnest. Playing at religion is wretched: it is everything or it is nothing.

Peace be with you all and abounding love

Your hearty friend

C. H. Spurgeon

Menton, 6th March [year not stated]

Beloved Friends,

I am most happy to have the prospect of speedily seeing you face to face, and of doing so with joy. The merciful hand of the Lord has restored me in body and mind, and I am very sanguine that for many a day I shall be able to labour among you without a breakdown similar to that which laid me aside. I have needed every day of rest which I have enjoyed, but it is a great delight to me to be near the close of my enforced silence and to have the prospect of again proclaiming 'the glorious gospel of the Blessed God'.

The success of the special services must have cheered you all, and now is the time while full of gratitude for the harvest, to see to the ingathering. The converts will need to be introduced to Christian fellowship, and then comforted and further instructed in the fear of the Lord. It will be our duty to maintain a warm temperature in the church for it would be very injurious for the little ones to be brought into an ice-house. We must all endeavour to make the church a happy home for the Lord's newborn ones and lay ourselves out to make them feel how welcome they are. I cannot suggest what each one can do but I may entreat each of my dear brethren and sisters to find out his or her own work, and set about it with that promptness and pleasure which are the very life of success. Let us all begin anew. The Pastor starts again, let all who have become backward or have felt incapable begin with him anew. 'The Lord has been mindful of us, he will bless us.'

I thank you for maintaining the offering for the College so long and so well. It is our chief way of spreading the gospel, and one of the best ever placed within the reach of Christian men. The sending forth of ministers in the name of the Lord touches the most vital point of the great cause and I, for one, feel that I cannot engage in a more useful work. Let us therefore, for a thousand reasons keep our

College well supplied, but especially for our own Lord's sake whose servants we endeavour to help.

Receive assurances of my continual memory of you all. I bear you on my heart. Peace be to you and peace be to your households.

Yours heartily

C. H. Spurgeon

Spurgeon photographed in later years

Menton, Wednesday evening [undated]

To my dear friends at the Tabernacle,

It is only a few days since I wrote you and therefore I have nothing fresh to report except that each day I feel the need and the value of the rest which I am beginning to enjoy. I have only arrived here this afternoon but the warm sunshine and the clear atmosphere make me feel as if I had reached another world, and tend greatly to revive a weary mind.

It would be well if I could write without a word of mention of myself, and for your edification only. Forgive the need which there is of my mentioning my health; it would best please me if I could work right on and never have the wretched item of self to mention. My mind runs much upon the work at home, the services, the College, the Orphanage, the Colportage, the Sabbath School, the coming meetings and so on. I picture all things in my mind's eye and wonder how all go on, and then pray and leave the whole with 'that great Shepherd of the sheep'. There is my brother too, and all the officers, they will watch for the good of the church, and the more spiritual and full grown among you – you also will care for the state of the work, and so the Lord will use your instrumentality for his glory. We are set for a sign and token of the power of the old-fashioned gospel, and we are bound to prove to all around not only that the truth can gather but that it can hold. It will not only forcibly draw men together but it will bind them together, and that too, not through some favoured preacher but by its own intrinsic force. This assertion needs proof and you will prove it.

May God, the Eternal Spirit, abide over you all, beloved, and cause you to be strong in the anointing of the Holy One. May the poor be comforted, the sick supported, the warriors be strengthened and the labourers be sustained. My hearty love is ever with you.

Yours in Christ Jesus

C. H. Spurgeon

Keep up the prayer meetings

BACKGROUND REGARDING THE ORPHANAGE

The Orphanage began in 1866 when a large donation was given by Mrs Anne Hillyard to house and educate orphan boys. In London at that time there were many thousands of destitute children who either died or went into a life of crime. A plot was purchased at Stockwell and built as a long row of individual homes each with a matron to be mother to the boys. Quite differently from contemporary institutions, it provided the boys with a large gymnasium, swimming pool, playing field and a hospital. Spurgeon took a great interest in the orphans, visiting them frequently and championing their needs to those able to support financially. The boys were from varied backgrounds. In 1877 a girls' orphanage was also built so there was now capacity for 250 boys and 250 girls. Spurgeon and his wife customarily had Christmas dinner with the orphans where the social pleasures of Christmas would be enjoyed – the children competitively decorating their respective homes and many gifts and special food such as figs and oranges given to them in response to Spurgeon's appeals in *The Sword and the Trowel*[*]. Many children were converted and some of the boys went on to the Pastors' College and to pastor churches or be missionaries. The letter below shows the happy interaction Spurgeon had with the orphans.

Menton, 23rd December 1883

Dear Children,

It pleases me to think of you all as full of glee and gladness today. Let us thank God for providing the Orphanage and then for giving us kind friends who think of our daily wants, and then again for finding another set of friends to make us merry on Christmas Day. You see the Lord not only sends us our daily bread, but something over. Let us together bless the Great Father's name. I do not know how you can thank him better than by becoming his own dear children, through believing in his Son Jesus. I hope every boy and girl will be ➤

[*]Eg: 'We must remind the good and the gracious that Christmas is coming – coming very soon. Now, there are 500 boys and girls, with their matrons and teachers, who live in a lovely place called Stockwell Orphanage; and Father Christmas, it is hoped, will look in upon them also. Now the aforesaid 500 do not want to keep the feast on bread and butter, or suet dumpling; but they would much better like roast beef and plum pudding, and some oranges and nuts, and – well, anything good will do! Will kind fathers, and mothers, and aunts and uncles who have their own dear ones to think of, also think of the Stockwellites, and send on a little something marked "for the Christmas treat"?' (December 1888)

> found believing in Jesus, loving Jesus, and serving Jesus.

I am just a thousand miles away from you, but my love gets to you by one great leap. It is a little after seven on Sabbath morning, the sun is just up, and the sea is like melted silver. There are such sweet roses in my room, and just outside the window there are oranges and lemons. Don't envy me, for I know the oranges are sour, and those which you will have today will be much better. Do not forget three cheers for Mr Duncan. I shall listen between 1 and 2 on Tuesday, and if I hear your voices I shall just ride on the moon to you, and drop down from the ceiling. That is a great big if! Be very happy and very kind to one another. Do not give the dear matrons and masters any trouble at any time. Obey immediately all Mr Charlesworth's rules, and make him happy, and then perhaps he will get quite stout.

God bless you, my dear girls and boys. Three cheers for the Trustees. No more, except my best love,

C. H. Spurgeon

Bird's-eye view of the Stockwell Orphanage

PART 2
1884-90

These seven years were a time of increased suffering, both physically and emotionally, as the Downgrade Controversy reared its head. In October 1887 Spurgeon led the Tabernacle out of the Baptist Union, and through *The Sword and the Trowel* magazine took a firm stand which attracted many attacks on him. This, he felt, intensified the severity of his health problems.

It was also a time of great blessing on the Tabernacle ministries, and hundreds of new converts were added to the church membership. Spurgeon finished *The Treasury of David* after 20 years, as well as other books, and his preaching ministry at home and elsewhere was maintained.

Menton, 10th January 1884

Dear Friends,

I am altogether stranded. I am not at all able to leave my bed, or to find much rest upon it. The pains of rheumatism, lumbago, and sciatica, mingled together, are exceedingly sharp. If I happened to turn a little to the right hand or to the left I am soon aware that I am dwelling in a body capable of the most acute suffering. However, I am as happy and cheerful as a man can be. I feel it such a great relief that I am not yet robbing the Lord of my work, for my holiday is not quite run out. A man has a right to have the rheumatism if he likes when his time is his own. The worst of it is that I am afraid that I shall have to intrude into my Master's domains, and draw again upon your patience. Unless I get better very soon I cannot get home in due time, and I am very much afraid that if I did get home at the right time I should be of no use to you, for I should be sure to be laid aside. The deacons have written me a letter in which they unanimously recommend me to take two more Sundays, so that I may get well, and not return to you an invalid. I wrote to them saying that I thought I must take a week, but as I do not get a bit better, but am rather worse, I am afraid I shall have to make it a fortnight, as they proposed. Most men find that they go right when they obey their wives, and as my wife and my deacons are agreed on this matter, I am afraid I should go doubly wrong if I ran contrary to them. I hope you will all believe that if the soldier could stand he would march, and if your servant were able he would work; but when a man is broken in two by the hammer of pain he must wait till he gets spliced again.

May the best of blessings continue to rest upon you. May those who supply my place be very graciously helped by the Spirit of God.

Yours with all my heart

C. H. Spurgeon

> This letter was written out by another hand and signed by Spurgeon. In January Spurgeon preached to a crowded French church in Menton. He was back preaching at the Tabernacle in February.

In 1884 special services were held to mark Spurgeon's 50th birthday. On June 17th 7,000 people were present at a meeting chaired by the Earl of Shaftesbury, when Spurgeon was given more than £4,500 which he distributed between the various departments of the work (and some to St Thomas' Hospital which assisted so many Tabernacle members). *The Times* noted on the occasion that 'the Metropolitan Tabernacle is probably the largest and best edifice for congregational worship in this country; our cathedrals being rather for spectacles, ceremonies, processions, and meditation…We are repeatedly told of tens of thousands whom it is impossible to get at, or to draw, or to interest in the affairs and prospects of their eternal souls. But it is quite plain by the facts before us that tens of thousands can be drawn, and secured too, in what used to be thought the most hopeless parts of the metropolis.'

On Christmas Day he dined with Mrs Spurgeon at the Orphanage, but this was to be the last time he was able to carry out this previously regular commitment.

Westwood, Beulah Hill, Upper Norwood
20th November 1885

Dear Brethren,

I thank you very much and if I find after Sunday that I am not able to go on I will give up at once; but I would greatly prefer to finish up in a fortnight without disappointing any one. I do not feel right but I think I can take a few more steps and complete the journey.

Yours lovingly
C. H. Spurgeon

(Portion of original of letter overleaf)

This last week has been one of great pain. One of its worst trials has been my inability to hold a pen. When I woke this morning & found that my right hand had become smaller & that I c'd write - I felt ready to cry for joy.

Westwood, Beulah Hill
Upper Norwood
16th May 1886

I am, your suffering servant for Christ's sake,
C.H. Spurgeon.

(Portion of original)

Dear Friends,

In answer to many prayers I was permitted three times to attend the conference: but possibly this great privilege, though it gave me much joy, also helped to prolong my affliction. Nevertheless I cannot feel too grateful for such special favour. Pray for a blessing on the conference. Ask the Lord to make our ministers sound in the faith.

This last week has been one of great pain. One of its worst trials has been my inability to hold a pen. When I woke this morning and found that my right hand had become smaller and that I could write – I felt ready to cry for joy. My first thought was to get up at once and write to you a word of sincere affection.

God bless you one and all, out of the eternal treasury of his love. O that my afflictions may make me a more profitable preacher to you! I would gladly suffer anything if I might more fully glorify God, and benefit his people, and save sinners.

I pray you to have patience with me under my many infirmities, and when I am once again among you, which I hope will be very soon, do hear me all you can while I am to be heard. I can truly say that when I can preach I throw my whole soul into it, and I feel anxious that as many as possible may hear what the Lord may speak through me. May the Holy Ghost make such hearing to be effectual unto salvation.

I think I shall this week issue my nineteen hundredth sermon. I have been thinking of 'Rejoice evermore' as a fit text. Brethren let us rejoice.

Hoping to be with you next Sabbath day,

I am, your suffering servant for Christ's sake,

C. H. Spurgeon

The following letter was read at the Tabernacle on Sunday 13th November 1887

Dear Friends at Tabernacle,

I have only left you a few days, but I am already rested by anticipation of rest to come. I wish to thank you all most heartily for your constancy of love during four and thirty years of fellowship. We have been many in number but only one in heart all through these years. Specially is this true in the present hour of controversy, for my heartiest sympathisers are in my own church. Several enthusiastic ones proposed a general meeting of church members to express their fervent agreement with their Pastor; but the ever faithful deacons and elders had taken time by the forelock, and presented to me a letter signed by them all as representing their brethren and sisters. Such unity comes from the grace of God, proves that his blessing is now with us, and prophesies future happiness. What can I do but thank you all, and love you in return, and labour for you as long as strength remains, and pray for you till I die? The infinite blessing of the Eternal God be with you for ever.

Your grateful Pastor

C. H. Spurgeon

This letter was written at the height of the Downgrade Controversy. On the reverse of this letter, written by another hand, is the following – 'We give the document alluded to in the above letter. It would have been worded far more strongly, but the Pastor is always for great brevity in expression concerning himself, and his wishes caused many a glowing paragraph to be struck out. There was a general feeling that the officers would like to have made the utterance more forcible; but they added that even then it would fall far short of the warmth of their feelings.'

That document, together with a further letter showing the great solidarity and affection with which the church stood behind the Pastor, is provided overleaf.

Two documents presented to Spurgeon in Menton showing the great solidarity and affection with which the church stood behind the Pastor during the Downgrade Controversy.

'Resolved:– "That we, the deacons and elders of the church, worshipping in the Metropolitan Tabernacle, hereby tender to our beloved Pastor, C. H. Spurgeon, our deep sympathy with him in the circumstances that have led to his withdrawal from the Baptist Union. And we heartily concur in our sincere appreciation of the steadfast zeal with which he maintains the doctrines of the gospel of our Lord Jesus Christ in their inspired and apostolic simplicity."

'Signed by the Co-Pastor, together with all the Deacons and Elders.'

'Our former resolution was passed with unanimous and unhesitating concurrence. But, touching only on one point, it was generally thought inadequate to convey to you, our dear Pastor, a full sense of the affection, the confidence, and the esteem in which you are held by us all. Of this, however, we can offer you no more fitting exposition than the readiness of each and every one to approve ourselves as "Helps" in the diversified gifts, administrations, and operations of the Holy Spirit with which you have, after the divine order, been so largely entrusted.

'And it may not be altogether inappropriate, or inopportune, to record our conviction that you have done good service, on a wide and constantly-widening scale, by affirming the inspiration of the Holy Scriptures of the Old and New Testament; by inculcating the doctrines of grace, as taught by the apostles of our Lord Jesus Christ under the immediate guidance of the Spirit of God; and by preserving in our midst the uncorrupted simplicity of public worship.

'Permit us to add our fervent hope, and our devout prayer, that your vigorous protests against the innovations of "modern thought" in pulpits supposed to be orthodox, will eventually largely promote the unity of the churches of Christ throughout the world.'

During the spring and summer of 1887 Spurgeon received fierce opposition for reiterating his warnings against false teaching in the ranks of the Baptist Union. A number of prominent ministers and college lecturers had embraced higher criticism, denying the infallibility and inerrancy of the Bible, and the Union leadership refused to respond to this 'downgrade' with any form of discipline to maintain the vital essentials of the faith. The crisis reached the point where he withdrew from the Baptist Union in October 1887. Spurgeon's stand for truth was wholly justified, because the Baptist Union, having become doctrinally comprehensive, steadily declined in biblical faithfulness from that time. Spurgeon wrote to a sympathiser –

'It was incumbent upon me to leave the Union, as my private remonstrances to officials, and my repeated pointed appeals to the whole body, had been of no avail…It is a great grief to me that hitherto many of our most honoured friends in the Baptist Union have, with strong determination, closed their eyes to serious divergences from truth. I doubt not that their motive has been in a measure laudable, for they desired to preserve peace, and hoped that errors, which they were forced to see, would be removed as their friends advanced in years and knowledge. But at last even these will, I trust, discover that the new views are not the old truth in a better dress, but deadly errors with which we can have no fellowship. I regard full-grown "modern thought" as a totally new cult, having no more relation to Christianity than the mist of the evening to the everlasting hills.' (Letter to Mr Mackey, 23rd November 1887.)

17th November 1887

To the Church at the Tabernacle,

Beloved Friends,

I write you because my heart prompts me to do so, and because many of you desire it. We have not been in hearty union for so many years without feeling a living interest in each other. This should be more largely the fruit of church membership than it usually is. The idea of real brotherhood should be more tenderly and more practically realised. Let us each one labour after it, and take a deep personal interest in our fellow members, especially in those who are poor, or ill, or young, or despondent, or under peculiar temptations and afflictions.

Thus should we make up among ourselves a sort of mutual pastorate, and should each gain as well as bestow a blessing. Because there is so much of this brotherly concern among you, I feel peace of heart while absent; but because there is not more of it I would stir up your pure minds by way of remembrance.

We are all the children of one Father, and redeemed with the precious blood of the same Saviour; let us therefore feel a natural instinct of unity, and from the force of the inner life cleave to each other in love. We are likely to need more and more that strength which comes from perfect unity of heart. Attacks will be made upon us by the forces of error, and we must stand shoulder to shoulder, or rather heart to heart, in the hour of conflict. May the Lord himself by his Holy Spirit enable us so to do!

My release from public service was greatly needed, for I have felt great prostration since last I wrote you. By your loving prayers I shall be strengthened, and enabled to use my rest for laying in new stores for future use. How much I desire that when I am again among you it may be in the fulness of the blessing of the gospel of peace!

I desire to be remembered to each one as truly as if I could grasp every hand, and say 'God bless you', to each individual.

Yours in Christ Jesus

C. H. Spurgeon

South of France
19th November [probably 1887]

Dear Friends,

At this time we have bad weather here, but the warmer climate shields us from the misery of mingled frost and fog. I have written a letter at some length to you, but I find that the printer has not space to put it in, and so to keep my word I must say a word or two; but necessity will allow no more.

I shall be greatly rejoiced if in my absence meetings for special prayer are called, and some extra work done for pressing the claims of the gospel upon the unconverted. What a joy it would be to hear that at the Tabernacle, and in all the churches of our beloved country, a revival of true religion had been wrought by the Spirit of God!

Seek this, and labour for it.

So pleads your loving friend

C. H. Spurgeon

Pastor Joseph W. Harrald, familiarly known as 'the armour-bearer', was private secretary to Spurgeon for many years. He was one of Spurgeon's most trusted friends. He devoted himself to help Spurgeon in his work. During the long illness of 1891, he kept everything in his sphere going – the letters, administration, editing of the weekly sermon and other literature work.

For many years he accompanied Spurgeon to Menton, and maintained the routine work of editing, and also the huge volume of correspondence. He had previously pastored a church in Shoreham for some years and then at Thornton Heath, but he resigned from pastoral ministry to assist Spurgeon fully. He preached in place of Spurgeon on several occasions and conducted the Sunday afternoon services in the Tabernacle lecture hall.

'Too familiar we, forget that he,
  Is the Reverend Joseph Harrald;
From Geneva he; his theology
  Is Calvinized and Farelled.'

C.H.S.

Menton

27th November 1887

To the Co-pastor and the Deacons,
My own dear brethren,

I am touched by your loving letter. It is just like you, but it is so tenderly, so considerately done, that it has a peculiar sweetness about it. May the Lord deal with each one of you as you have dealt towards me, even in tender love and true faithfulness!

See page 60 for the letter referred to here. Disapproval of Spurgeon's actions did lead to some withdrawing their financial support of the work, but others gave more generously. The controversy took its toll, Spurgeon writing, 'The strain has nearly broken my heart already, and I have had all I can bear of bitterness.' He received hundreds of supporting letters from ministers and clergymen around the country, including Bishop J. C. Ryle.

The more you know of this controversy, the more will your judgements go with me as well as your hearts. It is not possible for me to communicate to any one all that has passed under my knowledge; but I have had abundant reason for every step I have taken, as the day of days will reveal. All over the various churches there is the same evil, in all denominations in measure; and from all sorts of believers comes the same thankful expression of delight that the schemes of errorists have been defeated by pouring light upon them. I cannot at this present tell you what spite has been used against me, or you would wonder indeed; but the love of God first, and your love next, are my comfort and stay. We may, perhaps, be made to feel some of the brunt of the battle in our various funds; but the Lord liveth. Our great Dr Gill said, 'Sir, I can be poor, but I cannot sell my conscience,' and he has left his mantle as well as his chair in our vestry.

I should like to see you all walk in here, and hear your loving voices in prayer. Allison is a good representative, but he is not all of you, and I feel knit to you all more and more.

Yours for ever

C. H. Spurgeon

Menton
22nd December 1887

Dear Friends,

After the first Sabbath of 1888 is passed, I hope to see you face to face, and I trust I may have a message from my Master for you.

My rest has been of much service to me, and all the more so because it has placed me away from the immediate scene of a somewhat heated conflict. Perhaps the thoughts of men upon the serious matters involved will be none the worse for a little waiting. For my own part, I have not spoken without due consideration, and therefore I have chosen my ground, and by God's grace I shall maintain it against all comers, in the spirit of love, truth, but assuredly without vacillation. Continue your importunate prayers for me.

I am much concerned about our invaluable friend, Mr William Olney. We have aforetimes prayed him back from the gates of the grave; let us again plead for his restoration. O Lord, spare thy dear servant, for we need him greatly!

I wish you a very holy and happy Christmas with my loved and esteemed brother, Mr Davies. He is my true yoke-fellow. His Welsh fire will, I trust, warm your hearts if not your bodies. I can see snow out of my windows today, and the weather is cold and wet, so that we need a fire; but this is, I hope, only for a day or two, and then we shall be in summer shine again. If not, it will harden me off for coming back.

Please note that the sermon which completes two thousand comes out next week. I am specially grateful to the Lord for sparing me so long, and enabling me for so many years to issue a weekly sermon.

I desire hearty love to all my dear church and congregation.

'Stand fast in the Lord, my dearly beloved.'

Yours in eternal life

C. H. Spurgeon

Westwood, Beulah Hill, Upper Norwood
November 1888

Dear Friends,

So long as my enemy only punished my foot I could tread upon him, but when to great pain was added a general sense of being unwell, and I could no longer put my foot on the ground, I was obliged to give in. I think I have been highly favoured this year to have had so few breaks. I trust the Lord has made my ministry profitable among you. It might not have been so, had he not every now and then taught me personal lessons apart.

I hope, by God's blessing, to be all right by Sunday next, and possibly even by Thursday; but at present I cannot stand.

I am very sorry because there were only 3 Sabbaths before my departure and I wanted them to have been specially good. I pray that they may be better through the ministry of others than they would have been through mine. To one and all I send hearty love; and as I ask your prayers so do I affectionately pray – The Lord be with you.

Yours heartily

C. H. Spurgeon

On 14th November Spurgeon wrote in *The Sword and the Trowel* – 'Our grief is that we have been out of our pulpit, and away from our pastoral work during the three weeks which we hoped would have made the home vessel trim and tight, and prepared the crew to bear the captain's absence. Now we must go with many a matter out of order, many a purpose unfulfilled. Go we must, for it will not do to remain here, and neither do good nor get good. Since we cannot spend our strength, it must be wise to go where we can store it. The Lord, whom we serve, will not allow our unavoidable lack of service to be a serious injury to the church, which is his joy and care. Already showers of blessing are falling, and we leave amid a sound of abundance of rain.'

Menton
1st December 1888

Dear Friends,

Although we have had two days of rainy and tempestuous weather I have improved so greatly that I feel like the man who is described in Scripture as 'walking, and leaping, and praising God'. As I cannot quite manage the two former exercises I desire to be doubly abundant in the third. Watts says,

> When we are raised from deep distress
>   Our God demands a song;
> We take the pattern of our praise
>   From Hezekiah's tongue.

That man of God on his recovery said, 'The living, the living, he shall praise thee as I do this day.' In this spirit I have prepared a sermon to which this note is appended; and I have borne therein my willing testimony to the faithfulness of God, and to the certainty that he honours the faith of his people.

From the Tabernacle I have joyful news of a meeting at which four or five hundred persons came together to confess that they had found mercy during the late services. What a cordial to one's head! 'Therefore we will sing my songs to the stringed instruments all the days of our life in the house of the Lord.' Blessed be his name!

With my heart's best wishes for all my hearers and readers,

Their servant for Jesus Christ's sake

C. H. Spurgeon

In the December 1888 *Notes* of *The Sword and the Trowel* Spurgeon wrote: 'The Tabernacle mission commenced with three crowded services, and every week-night up to the time of writing, the vast building has been nearly filled…This result has been attained by a house-to-house visitation throughout the whole region round the Tabernacle by a noble band of between four and five hundred earnest Christian brethren and sisters, under the leadership of our esteemed elders…Our earnest prayer is, that the revival may continue until the whole of London is affected by it…A wind from the Spirit of God would be the surest method of blowing away the pestilential clouds of the "Down-Grade".'

Westwood, Beulah Hill, Upper Norwood
9th November 1890

Dear Friends,

How much I wish that I could have held out till this day. But last Sunday night my coach turned over and all the four horses went down. I have had a week of special pain, sleeplessness, and unrest of brain. These evils will soon be gone, now that I am to have a season of rest. There are so very many matters pressing upon me incessantly when I am in the work that I get brain-weary. I have had too much of late.

I did not sit down this morning to tell of my woes, but to thank you all, and specially to thank the Lord. I could not see you on Friday, but you brought what was needed all the same, and £100 more. Never people responded more heartily, lovingly, and generously. Each one gave according to his means. You saw it needful, and you did it for the Lord's sake.

You have made me very glad and almost proud: only when you have an aching head, one cannot come to be exalted above measure. Accept my loving thanks. Best of people, God bless you all.

Your grateful Pastor
C. H. Spurgeon

Spurgeon wrote these words about his coach as a metaphor of his sudden illness, but it was widely reported as a literal event. He wrote: 'It never entered my head that it could be taken literally. The season of the year was not suitable for coach-riding, and unhappily it is a pastime in which a London minister is at any season very rarely privileged to indulge... the world is so fond of fiction that anything will suffice as material to be hammered into a tale...Moral – Believe not one-half that you hear.' Spurgeon soon left for Menton after months of fruitful work.

On the Friday referred to in the letter Tabernacle friends had been invited to come and say goodbye to the Pastor and to contribute to the £1,000 needed for the cleaning and repair of the building. Spurgeon was unable to be present due to his illness, but a steady stream of members came regardless and a telegram was sent to Spurgeon in the evening telling him that the amount needed had been more than met.

Menton
15th November 1890

Dear Friends,

By God's goodness, though compassed with infirmity, I have preached right on through the year, although I have felt gradually growing feeble. During the last week of the term I was obliged to keep my bed: the body was in pain, and the mind could not work. It was a general running down of all my powers.

So I left home thoroughly exhausted and the journey to this delightful haven is a long one; but sitting here in the warm, clear sunlight, I feel that I am none the worse for the thousand miles of travelling. The change in climate is almost beyond belief. A few days in such air as this will set me up. What a change from being steamed to death in the almost solid fogs of London! Thanks be unto God for such a place of recovery for those who are spent in service! I would get out of it all the benefit I can, that my ministry may show vigour of mind and power of divine grace.

Bright upon the tablet of my heart is the record of what was done by Tabernacle friends on Friday, Nov. 7*; when the people willingly offered of their substance unto the Lord, and all that was needed for the repair of the house of our assembly was brought in at one stroke. A thousand times do I thank all those generous givers. Outside friends have also sent in grand amounts to provide for the other funds and thus the Lord has put his servant beyond care for the needs of the work at this present.

During his absence the Tabernacle was cleaned and repaired.
*See previous page for a note on this.

I write because continually requested to do and to assure you of my love in Christ Jesus.

Yours truly
C. H. Spurgeon

Menton
4th December 1890

Dear Friends,

I pray that while you are in two bands you may have a double blessing. May the Lord, who has been our guide and our glory all these years, sanctify these broken weeks to an increase of his manifested power!

For me there are many reasons for humble gratitude, – chiefly that I am free from pain, and I can use my hand a little though it is swollen, and writing cannot be long continued. I see that if we are puffed up we cannot work. If our trials prevent this evil, they are a great benefit to us. I seek a constant interest in your prayer. If it were the Lord's will, I could fain be well and strong, and then get rested, and be home with you again.

I send my love to all friends in Christ Jesus.

Yours very heartily

C. H. Spurgeon

The orphans on Founder's Day 1894

Menton
6th December 1890

Beloved Friends,

Up to this date I have had no opportunity to enjoy rest, but have been at first suffering, and now slowly recovering. This, however, is not lost time if I have but grace to improve the trials. Let us always seek sanctification through affliction rather than escape from it.

I have no question that there is great wisdom in the Lord's laying aside his instruments. It is for his own glory, for thereby he shows that he is not in need of them; and it is for their humbling, for hereby they learn how deep is their need of him. The uninterrupted reception of blessing through one channel might breed in our foolish hearts an idolatrous confidence in the means; therefore there comes a break in the use of the means that the Lord may be the more tenderly remembered. We may be sure that, if the Lord dries up a cistern, it is because he would have us fly to the fountain of inexhaustible strength.

I desire to rejoice that, in all these thirty-six years, with sicknesses so frequently upon me, I have never been compelled to drop either the weekly sermon or the monthly magazine. There has either been an interval of power, or I have been a little forward with the work when the stroke has laid me aside. May I not say 'Hitherto hath the Lord helped me'? Having received help of God, I continue unto this day; and I shall abide in my calling so long as there is work for me to do for my Lord.

I send my loving Christian salutations, to all my hearers and ➤

Soon after Spurgeon's death, Dr Pierson estimated that the printed sermons had reached between 20,000,000 and 40,000,000 readers, commenting that they had been 'translated into 23 tongues and dialects that we know of – French, Italian, Spanish, German, Dutch, Swedish, Russian, Chinese, Japanese, Syriac, Arabic, South American tongues, those of the islands of the South Seas, of the continents of Asia, of Africa, and of Europe.'

➤ readers, with earnest request for their prayers for myself personally, and for a blessing upon the sermons, and all the work at the
Metropolitan Tabernacle.

The times are out of course; the walls of human confederacies are
crumbling; the fashion of this world is passing away; 'but the Word
of the Lord endureth for ever, and this is the Word which by the
gospel is preached unto you.'

Yours in loving service for our Lord Jesus

C. H. Spurgeon

PART 3
1891-2
The final year

Spurgeon spent the early weeks of 1891 in Menton. He was well enough to lead daily devotions, expounding *Genesis* each morning to up to 60 people, some walking miles to be there. He returned to the Tabernacle in February, feeling a degree of health and vigour. His itinerary was filled with special meetings. In April and May he presented 84 new candidates for membership, and chaired and preached at the College Conference.

He presided over the annual church meeting for the last time in 1891. At this meeting it was reported that the membership was 5,328; the church had 127 lay ministers serving in and around London; the people of the Tabernacle were operating 23 mission buildings having a total of 4,000 seats; and were running 27 Sunday Schools ministering to 8,000 children, and engaging 600 teachers. Surrey Gardens Memorial Hall seating 1,000 was soon to be opened.

On 7th June he preached at the Tabernacle for the last time, and by the end of that month was extremely ill. The Tabernacle held an all-day prayer meeting lasting 14 hours on 29th June. Many people of all denominations sent letters of good wishes, as did many in public life including the Prince of Wales, and the former Prime ➤

➤ Minister, W. E. Gladstone. Twice daily prayer meetings continued as the illness was diagnosed as Bright's Disease (chronic nephritis).

A remarkable degree of recovery followed and by August Spurgeon was able to write again (see his letter to the congregation on page 98).

He went to Menton at the end of October as Dr A. T. Pierson arrived to assist in the Tabernacle work.

Spurgeon seemed much better and resumed speaking to small groups in France, and writing. He had the delight of three months in Menton with his wife as she was well enough to travel with him this time.

On New Year's Eve he gave a short address at his hotel (see page 124), and again the next day. The last hymn he gave out was on 17th January – 'The sands of time are sinking.'

His last days were spent only partly conscious, and on 31st January 1892 he was called home to glory. The Tabernacle received the telegram telling them that – 'Our beloved Pastor entered Heaven eleven five Sunday night.'

Menton
12th January 1891

To the Church Officers,
My Beloved Brethren,

Another death among us, too soon! It is a loud voice to us all to stand ready.

I greatly wish I had been at home, for Mr Carr was an old comrade, and perhaps better known and valued by me than by anyone else, – since he served me in many private literary ways. He was true as steel to the old faith, and to me as an advocate of it. He was eccentric in manner, but in doctrine he kept to the form of sound words with great firmness.

I am sure you will in my absence do all that the severe weather allows to make the family and the world see how we respect an ancient comrade, and a brother-officer.

Some letters of sympathy would come well from you as a body of deacons and elders: but this you will have thought of apart from my suggestion.

Also pray for Mrs Carr, with that large family, and so many of them young men or boys. What a charge for her! The Lord bless them!

Hearing of the continued badness of the weather, I accept the advice telegraphed by deacons, and supported by letters from many valued friends, and I will remain here another week, – not idle, but storing powder and shot for the fight.

Brethren, you know I love you, and I know the same of you.
Yours in Christ Jesus
C. H. Spurgeon

B. Wildon Carr was a deacon at the Tabernacle and had been a close friend of Spurgeon for many years. In a church the size of the Tabernacle, many members died each year – 74 dying the year this letter was written out of a membership of 5,328. Speaking of the home call of several key workers that year, Spurgeon said, 'Our heart would tremble at the thought of the departure of such friends, did we not rest in the living God, whose everlasting purposes secure a succession of saintly men and women who will carry on his work below.'

Menton
15th January 1891

My Dear Friends,

I have accepted the advice of the deacons, and of a number of friends who write with loving anxiety for my welfare, and I will remain here one week longer than I had purposed. I joyfully expect, if the Lord will, to be in your midst on Feb. 8. May it be as much a blessing to you as it will be a privilege to me! By your kind consideration I have been afforded a long rest, and I hope to have a proportionately long period of service as the result of it. My position is one which involves great wear and tear of mind and heart, and I am not now the youth I was when I became minister of your church 37 years ago, and hence I value your kindness in affording me the rest.

Alas, I shall not again see on earth all I left when I quitted your shores. I will not attempt to name the holy men and women who have gone home. Their monuments are in my heart. May the mourners be comforted! We shall meet the dear ones in Immanuel's Land.

It is well that on Feb. 1 you should hear my good friend, Mr Stott, who is, I hope sent to us of the Lord to help me in the work. He has gathered many to the Saviour and it will be a grand beginning of his coming among us if the first Sabbath should be a day of soul-winning. So may it be! I am grateful to Mr Robertson for coming a second time to the Tabernacle. The Lord make him a mighty man for the defence of the truth!

Now peace be on you all, and grace, from God our Father, and our Lord Jesus Christ! I pray that we may now begin a new era. May frost and fog be gone from the churches as well as from the streets; and may we see truth triumphant, grace victorious, and the Lord himself exalted!

Yours ever lovingly
C. H. Spurgeon

Menton
22nd January 1891

Beloved Friends,

I trust that by this time the weather has changed with you, since we have a decided improvement here. Continue to remember the poor. It has been a heavy trial for our country to have nearly two months of frost. Well did the Psalmist say, 'Who can stand before HIS cold?' Even here the more delicate plants and trees look as if a hot iron had been passed over them, and others are quite burned up with the extreme cold, – I know not how else to describe it.

I am glad that I am so near returning to you, for I am feeling ready and even eager to engage once more in the happy work of proclaiming the gospel to the crowd. This week's printed sermon will assure you that I stand by the old standard; and I am all the more bound to do so when I note the new developments of error, of which I am bound to say that they seem from different points of view as horrible as ludicrous. There is no telling what we shall hear next: but Jesus Christ is the same yesterday, today, and for ever.

Pray ye the Lord of the harvest to send forth labourers into his harvest, and to stop those who sow tares among the wheat. I ask your hearty aid in the College work. Just now the streams which supply it are frozen up, but as it is the Lord's work I know it cannot fail. Still, we must think of it.

I trust Mr Stott will be anointed among us for great usefulness in following up some things which, from want of strength, I have been obliged to withhold myself. Have special prayer for him, and for me also, that I may enjoy liberty in speaking among you, and may receive guidance in the work of the Lord.

Peace be to you and to your households! May the sun shine, and the warm winds blow, and the voice of the turtle be heard in the land!

Yours in intense union of heart

C. H. Spurgeon

Menton
Thursday 29th January 1891

Dear Friends,

I hope this is the last letter I shall send home this time, and that on Feb. 8 I shall be among you in person. I cannot be sure of anything, for on Tuesday I suddenly suffered a severe attack of my terrible enemy, and I am not yet clear of it, though making desperate efforts to shake off the foe. I have a firm confidence that I shall return on the appointed day, and shall be with you when expected; yet I would that you should ask this of the Lord for me, for I am not well just now.

I go this morning to preach at the opening of the Presbyterian Chapel; and though physically unfit, I believe I shall be helped. When I have performed my work, I will finish this note, and tell you how I have felt.

I have been enabled to bear testimony to a large assembly to 'redemption through his blood, the forgiveness of sins, according to the riches of his grace'. I felt it hard to stand, but joyful work to speak, though my voice was somewhat poor through weakness.

I cannot longer be silent. In this place I have received many letters from persons who have found Christ through my ministry in days gone by, and therefore I must again be at my life-work.

I am already mending, and hope to be clear of the lion which has leaped on the horse's back. You will understand the simile.

May Mr Stott have a great haul with his big net on both occasions on the Sabbath! My love is with you all, and I am glad that the Arctic time now gives place to a more temperate season in the weather. May it be as the Torrid Zone as to gracious warmth!

Yours in Christ for ever

C. H. Spurgeon

BACKGROUND TO THE LAST FULL YEAR

Spurgeon was back in the pulpit at the Tabernacle on 8th February. Mr Stott, mentioned in the last three letters, had been appointed an assistant minister in the year 1891, Spurgeon having written to him – 'It would be a great relief to me if I knew that someone was on the spot to take the pulpit should I suddenly fail.'

The College Conference was held 20th-24th April, during which Spurgeon gave the well-known call to the old faith – 'The Greatest Fight in the World'. Spurgeon wrote: 'The week of the conference was one of exhausting delight…of course there was a reaction for the one who was at the centre of all this; and for the first time in a ministry of forty years, we entered the pulpit on the Sunday evening *[17th May]*, and were obliged to hurry out of it; for a low, nervous condition shut us up. Happily, Mr Stott could take up the story there and then…how great is the foresight of the Lord in sending us such a helper.'

The week prior to this had been a gruelling one with many extra preaching engagements at special meetings both at the Tabernacle and elsewhere in addition to the regular sermons, editing and appointments. After this he became ill with what was thought to be influenza.

Throughout this year, Spurgeon was continuing the fight against the downgrade of the faith. Combating those who were saying he had overreacted, he wrote in *The Sword and the Trowel* of June 1891 –

> 'The idea that loose theology is quitting the denominations is a fiction… Ministers have quoted, with very slight censure, books which are ruining the souls of men, and the guilt lies at their door. That there is no increase to the churches is perhaps one of the least of many evils; but were the hearts of Christians in a right state, it would be viewed as a calamity calling for days of humiliation and prayer. Instead of this, the progress to infidelity goes on rapidly, and ministers and laymen alike are content to have it so.'

Westwood, Beulah Hill, Upper Norwood
23rd May 1891

Dear Friends,

My doctor will not allow me to leave my bedroom on any pretence whatever. He thinks me better, but says I must not go out for days to come.

I do not propose to put off the collections for the Surrey Memorial, because your love is just as generous in my absence as in my presence. I want some £270 now to complete the £3000 which the ground and buildings have cost. You will not allow me to have any trouble about that.

I would be among you to tell you all about it, but the doctor says I shall not do anything of the sort, and he is a man of peculiarly strong will. He searched me and sounded me at the first, and shut me up all the week; and he was right. I might have been among the departed if he had not taken me in time, and finding me down with chill, nursed me for a while. He has been here three times a day all along, and I am grateful for his care.

The Surrey Gardens Memorial Hall (seating 1000) was to be a memorial of his ministry in the Surrey Gardens Music Hall, and also to assist the Carter Street Sunday School. Spurgeon was very disappointed not to be able to preach at the opening.

If this amount is supplied while I am ill, I shall come out with a doubly smiling face. I think it goes to be done if a few resolve that it shall be: in fact, it is done if you all say it must be.

Hoping soon to be at large again, but grateful to be yet alive.

I am
Your loving Pastor
C. H. Spurgeon

Final year letters continue on page 97

Westwood
Beulah Hill
Upper Norwood
1891 Aug 9

Dear Brethren,

The Lord's name be praised for first giving & then hearing the loving prayers of his people. Through these prayers my life is prolonged. I feel greatly humbled, + very grateful at being the object of so great a love + so wonderful an outburst of prayer.

I have not strength to say more . — Let the name of the Lord be glorified. Yours most heartily

C.H. Spurgeon

The first letter written after the long illness of 1891. See page 98.

Westwood
Beulah Hill
Upper Norwood
May 16 1886

Dear Friends

In answer to many prayers I was
permitted three times to attend the
Conference : but possibly this
gt privilege, though it gave me much
joy, also helped to prolong my affliction.
Nevertheless I cannot feel too grateful
for such special favour. Pray for a
blessing on the Conference, Ask the Lord
to make our ministers sound in the faith,

This last week has been one of gt
pain. One of its worst trials has been my
inability to hold a pen — When I woke
this morning & found that my right hand had
become smaller & that I cd write — I
felt ready to cry for joy : My first

thought was to get up at once & write to you a word of sincere affection.

God bless you one & all, out of the eternal treasury of his love. O that my afflictions may make one a more profitable preacher to you! I wd gladly suffer anything if I might more fully glorify God, & benefit his people, & save sinners.

I pray you to have patience with me under my many infirmities, & when I am once again among you, which I hope will bee very soon, do hear me all you can while I am to bee heard. I can truly say that when I can preach I throw my whole soul into it, & I feel anxious that as many as possible may hear what the Lord may speak through me. May the Holy Ghost make such hearing to bee effectual unto Salvation.

I think I shall this week issue my <u>nineteen hundredth sermon</u>. I have been thinking of "Rejoice evermore" as a fit text, Brethren let us rejoice.

Hoping to bee with you next Sabbath day,

I am, your suffering servant for Christ's sake,
C. H. Spurgeon.

See page 58

Cannes
Jan 31

To my beloved Church
+ Congregation,

Dear Friends,

The journey here is long
for one who is in weak health, &
I have had but a few days of
rest, but already I feel myself
improving. The Master's service
among you has been very delightful
to me, but it has grown to such
proportions that I have felt the burden
of it upon my spirits, & I have
suffered more depression of heart,
& weariness of mind than I could
well express. Rest I could not
find at home, where every hour
has its cares; but here I cease
altogether from these things & the
mind becomes like an unstrung
bow, & so regains its elasticity.
I wish I could work on among
you continually & never even pause
but many infirmities show that
this cannot be. Pray therefore
that this needful break in my

work may strengthen me for a long spring & summer campaign.

Nothing can so cheer me as to know that all of your are living for Jesus & living like him. Our church has produced great workers in the past & I hope the sacred enthusiasm wh they manifested will never burn low among us. Jesus is worth being served with our best, yea with our all, & that in an intense & all-consuming manner. May our young men & women love the Lord much & win others to him by their zeal for God, & may our elder brethren & the matrons among us prove ever the pillars of the Church in their holy conversation & devout godliness.

Maintain the prayermeetings at blood-heat. See well to the schools & all the classes, & other labours for Xt. Let nothing flag of prayer, service, or offering. We have a great trust, may the Lord make us faithful to it.

My love is with you all & my prayers for your welfare.

O that you who are still unsaved may be led to Jesus through those who supply my lack of service. Peace with the copastor, deacons & elders & with you all from your loving but unworthy Pastor

C. H. Spurgeon

See page 23

Menton. Nov. 27. 87.

To the Co-pastor & the Deacons,

My own dear brethren,

I am touched by your loving
letter. It is just like you, but it is
so tenderly, so considerately done, that
it has a peculiar sweetness about it.
May the Lord deal with each one of you
as you have dealt towards me, even in
tender love & true faithfulness!
The more you know of this controversy, the more
will your judgments go with me as well
as your hearts. It is not possible for
me to communicate to any one all that
has passed under my knowledge; but
I have had abundant reason for every
step I have taken, as the day of days
will reveal. All over the various churches
there is the same evil, in all denominations
in measure; & from all sorts of believers
comes the same thankful expression
of delight that the schemes of errorists
have been defeated by pouring light upon
them.

I cannot at this present tell you what spite has been used against me, or you would wonder indeed; but the love of God first, your love next, are my comfort & stay. We may, perhaps, be made to feel some of the brunt of the battle in our various funds; but the Lord liveth. One great Dr Gill said, "Sir, I can be poor, but I cannot sell my conscience", & he has left his mantle as well as his chair in our vestry.

I should like to see you all walk in here, & hear your loving voices in prayer. Allison is a good representative, but he is not all of you, & I feel knit to you all more & more.

Yours for ever

C. H. Spurgeon

This letter was written at the height of the Downgrade Controversy. See page 64.

Westwood
Beulah Hill
Upper Norwood
1891 Sep 13

Dear Friends,

I cannot write much but
cannot withhold my heart + my
pen from saying "O bless the Lord
with me & let us exalt his name
together". This week has by its
fine weather set me free from a
3 months's captivity. Those believers
of all denominations who so lovingly
prayed for me will now help
me to praise the Lord. Verily the
living God heareth prayer.

I fear my doctors would have a
mournful tale to tell of my disease

& from inward consciousness I must agree with them; but I feel better & I get into the open air & therefore I hope my face is turned toward recovery. Reading, writing, thinking &c are not yet easy to me — I am forced to vegetate. I fear it will be long before I can be at my beloved work. I send my hearty love to you all, & my humble gratitude to that great army of praying people who have been heard of the Lord in their cries for the prolongation of my life. May we believe more, pray more, & therefore receive more. Yours in bonds of true affection

C. H. Spurgeon

Written after the long illness of 1891. See page 99.

Menton Dec 10. 91

Beloved Friends,

Every message from home concerning
the work at the Tabernacle comforts me.
Your unity of heart, & prayerfulness of spirit,
are a joy to me. How much I wish that
I could look you in the face, & lead you
in prayer to the throne of the heavenly grace.

I am, however, glad that I am not yet
standing on the platform among you attempting
public prayer, or address, for emotion would carry me
away, & I sh.ᵈ soon be quite exhausted.
I put this to practical proof by offering prayer
with some six or seven friends: I was
overcome & was some time before I c.ᵈ recover
myself. Still the mind is ready, & the
physical frame must in due time follow
the road to restoration; indeed I feel
better, & have no fear but in due season
I shall be as strong as aforetime.

It is not in my power to hasten to

strength
~~health~~ : this must come by degrees as
the Lord may please to grant it. Pray
for me that the time be not too long.

I want all those who take an interest
in Tabernacle work to see that the funds
are all right at the close of the year.
My absence has tried the home cause very
much, & I hope that every one will resolve
that no deficiency shall occur in anything,
for that will be a great grief to me. Be
thoughtfully generous just now & it
will be most seasonable. We must
never allow home funds to be straitened,
                    personally
while we receive so freely of the grace of God.

Mr Spurgeon & myself are happy to be privileged
                                    we are
to be together in this ~~sunny~~ land; (both of us full
of gratitude that we are spared to each other, & both
thankful to you for remembering us in y prayers.
God bless you each one
                    Yours ever heartily
                              C H Spurgeon

Menton. Dec. 17. 1891.

My Dear Friends,

[Though I cannot be present to wish you the blessings of the season, I would not use the words of compliment, but I would say from my heart "I wish you a most happy Christmas". Upon your family gatherings may the best blessing rest! May all your children be the Lord's children, & thus may your union in the bonds of the flesh be made eternal by the bonds of the Spirit! Joy be with you: yet let it be joy in the Lord.

I would beg you to remember my orphan charge, & make them merry on the day of the feast. Remember also the poor, & let no one lack if you are able to relieve or to help in doing so.

I think I can fairly say, — I am better. Whether or no the Disease is disappearing, I cannot say, though I fear there is not much difference; but in general health I must be improved, or else my feelings are sheer delusion. At any rate, I am very hopeful, and praiseful, & I wish I could stand up, & give out Psalm CIII.

The blessing of the Father, the Son, & the Holy Ghost be with each one of you, evermore!

Yours most heartily

C. H. Spurgeon

See page 114

II Kings V. 11. "Behold I thought"

Our great aim is conversion for graves are filling on all
sides. For the present distress it is demanded that we
give ourselves mainly to this work.
Preconceptions are great enemies to faith even in
believers. We judge as to how the Lord will deal with us
on the road to heaven. How he will answer prayer.
How he will sanctify affliction. We even judge
against his promises & say "all these things are against me"
or else for our own ease "my mountain standeth firm"
The profession of a prophet does not suit us.

Preconceptions are great enemies to seekers.
Sinners awakened desire healing but they have ways of
their own marked out.

1. How do you expect to know by thought?
   Could you foresee the action of a physician?
   If it be so what need of a revelation?
   To what end is the Spirit of God given?
   Where have yr thoughts already landed you?

2. Should the arrangement of God be according to yr mind!
   Is he not rightly a sovereign in this matter?
   Is he not far wiser than yourself?
   Would it not feed yr selfconceit if —?
   Would it not derogate from the glory of God?

3. By what rule can you preconceive
   By what you wish?
   By yr own understanding? "as high as the heavens"
   By religious notions inherited?
   By what you have read or observed?
   By the ideas current in Society?

4. How would it be if it were as you thought?
   Do you expect peace by undergoing a ceremony?
   Do you wish to be saved by good works?
   Do you want pardon without atonement?

Must you needs experience great horrors?
8. you stipulate for raptures & excitements?
Did you hope to work yrself up by your own efforts?

5. To what do you object?
It seems so mysterious!
It looks like nothing at all!
It makes one into a mere child!
It throws the whole thing so open!
It implies so much against me!
It gives one nothing to be proud of!

6. Will you perish sooner than accept God's way?
It will not alter for you.
It will always involve the same necessity
You increase yr guilt & punishment.
You will certainly get no comfort out of yr folly.
To be lost for a whim will be insanity!

7. Will you not even now obey?
It is simple.
It asks nothing from you.
It is most fitting that you shd trust.
The result is certain, immediate,
effectual, eternal.

34 Evan
560 Belmont.
533

Spurgeon's evangelistic sermon notes for Sunday May 17th 1874.

Menton. Nov. 15. 90.

Dear Friends,

By God's goodness, though compassed with infirmity, although I have preached right on through the year, but I felt gradually growing feeble. During the last week of the term I was obliged to keep my bed: the body was in pain, & the mind at not work. It was a generally running down of all my powers. So I left home thoroughly exhausted. the journey to this delightful haven is a long one; but sitting here in 1 warm, clear, sunlight, I feel that I am none the worse for the thousand miles o travelling. the change in climate is almost beyond belief. A few days in such air as this will set me up. What a change from being steamed to death in 1 almost solid fog of London! Thanks be unto God for such a place o recovery for those who are spent in service! I would get out of it all 1 benefit I can, t my ministry may show vigour o mind + power o divine grace.

Bright upon 1 tablet of my heart is 1 record o what was done by Tabernacle friends on Friday, Nov. 7, when the people willingly offered o their substance unto the Lord, & all t was needed for 1 repair of 1 house o our assembly was brought in at one stroke. A thousand times do I thank all those generous givers. Outside friends have also sent in grand amounts to provide for the other funds t 1 Lord has put his servant beyond care for the needs of the work at this present.

I write because continually requested to do, to assure you of my love in Christ Jesus. yours truly C. H. Spurgeon

See page 69

Westwood, Beulah Hill, Upper Norwood
31st May 1891

Dear Friends,

The mysterious disease which brought me into such great dangers has now left me very weak. The doctor thinks there would be peril in my coming out to speak on Tuesday, and so we must postpone opening the Memorial.

Next Sunday I hope I may get permission for one service at least. I am thankful to be permitted to work on with you here below a little longer, and as soon as I can gather a little strength I will see enquirers and make up for lost time. Do pray for me. There must be a reason for my having passed through that narrow pass in which so many have fallen. I never dreamed of such a thing when I spoke with you last: I only knew that a fixed heavy headache pressed me down. That headache has not quite gone yet; but the brain is recovering.

I want you to aid me in clearing off what is now wanted for the Memorial. I think £100 would be the end of it: and I am laid aside that this stone may be rolled away from that beautiful edifice.

The Lord bless the pastors who preach today; and may I live to see you in your full number next Lord's Day.

Yours ever heartily

C. H. Spurgeon

Spurgeon did preach on 7th June as he had hoped in this letter, but on 12th his health broke down completely.

That sermon was to be his last at the Metropolitan Tabernacle, after almost 38 years as Pastor.

(Portion of original)

As Spurgeon entered a phase of severe illness with long periods of delirium, the Tabernacle and countless other Christians began a prolonged time of special prayer. Doctors now confirmed the diagnosis as Bright's Disease. Mrs Spurgeon wrote – 'The Tabernacle Church beginning with a whole day of intercession for the suffering Pastor, continued to meet, morning, noon, and night, to plead for his recovery. In hundreds and perhaps thousands of Nonconformist places of worship, sympathetic petitions were presented on his behalf.' It has already been noted that letters and telegrams were received from a huge number of people (the local telegraph office broke down) including messages from the Prince of Wales, several of the nobility as well as those from the Established Church. By 9th August he was well enough to write the letter below, but prayer meetings at the Tabernacle continued twice daily.

Westwood, Beulah Hill, Upper Norwood
9th August 1891

Dear Brethren,

The Lord's name be praised for first giving and then hearing the loving prayers of his people. Through these prayers my life is prolonged. I feel greatly humbled and very grateful at being the object of so great a love and so wonderful an outburst of prayer.

I have not strength to say more – let the name of the Lord be glorified.

Yours most heartily

C. H. Spurgeon

(Portion of original)

Westwood, Beulah Hill, Upper Norwood
13th September 1891

Dear Friends,

I cannot write much but I cannot withhold my heart and my pen from saying 'O bless the Lord with me and let us exalt his name together.' This week has by its fine weather set me free from a 3 months' captivity. Those believers of all denominations who so lovingly prayed for me will now help me to praise the Lord. Verily the living God heareth prayer.

I fear my doctors would have a mournful tale to tell of my disease and from inward consciousness I must agree with them; but I feel better and I get into the open air and therefore I hope my face is turned towards recovery. Reading, writing, thinking etc are not yet easy to me. I am forced to vegetate. I fear it will be long before I can be at my beloved work.

I send my hearty love to you all, and my humble gratitude to that great army of praying people who have been heard of the Lord in their cries for the prolongation of my life. May we believe more, pray more, and therefore receive more.

Yours in bonds of true affection

C. H. Spurgeon

(Portion of original)

I cannot write much but I cannot withhold my heart & my pen from saying "O bless the Lord with me & let us exalt his name together":

Westwood, Beulah Hill, Upper Norwood
27th September 1891

Dear Friends,

Every time I see a church officer I am cheered by tidings of your good condition as a church and people. In this there is joy to me. May our Lord keep us evermore united in love, fervent in prayer, and diligent in service.

As for myself, I have made no progress this week; but have rather gone backward than forward. When a man cannot eat how can he gather strength? I should have left home for the seaside if I had felt equal to the effort; but I am without energy, and must stay where I am. O that I could be among you! But I must be patient, and wait our Father's will. Your prayers included health and strength for me, and these I shall yet have, for mere life is scarcely a blessing without them. May I beg you to continue in supplication? I am sure you will.

If sharp pruning makes fruit-bearing branches bring forth more fruit it is not a thing to be lamented when the great Vine-dresser turns his knife upon us. If I may in the end be more useful to you, and to those who come in and out among us I shall rejoice in the woes which I have endured. May you each one when tried with sickness improve your school-time that you may be the sooner able to learn and know all the Master's mind.

God bless you this day by my dear brother A. G. Brown. May he be happy in your midst, and may God be glorified. Few are the men like-minded with Mr Brown, a brother tried and proved. Peace be to you and to your families.

Yours most lovingly
C. H. Spurgeon

Westwood, Beulah Hill
Upper Norwood
3rd October 1891

This trip to Eastbourne from 3rd-16th October was an experiment to see if he could bear the journey to Menton, as the doctors wanted him to spend the winter there to avoid the cold weather. The trip benefited him and he left for Menton on 26th October.

Dear Friends,

I write a line on Saturday because the bright sun has tempted me to get to the seaside, and I could not write you in time if I did not write now. As I have lost almost entirely my powers of eating, I feel it is time to do something, and I steal away to the sea in the hope that God will there revive me.

Your sacred unity and zeal are daily a comfort to me. Oh that I could be well, and serve you without a pause; but perhaps I am worth all the more as a worker because I have so fully been a sufferer. I am sure you will continue your prayers for me. May our God bless every one of you!

Yours most lovingly

C. H. Spurgeon

(Portion of original)

Westwood, Beulah Hill, Upper Norwood
18th October 1891

To my Beloved flock at Metropolitan Tabernacle
Dear Friends,

   Since you all prayed for me so importunately I would entreat you to praise with me most heartily. My stay by the sea has wrought wonders: I feel a different man altogether, and my doctor gives me hope that when I have received a solid upbuilding I shall not be much the worse for the terrific processes through which I have passed. 'O magnify the Lord with me and let us exalt his name together.' I am very very weak, and restoration to strength must be expected to be gradual. The inevitable fall of the temperature is a great peril to me, for several reasons, and hence my medical friend wishes that I were away. I hope to leave on Monday 26. Pray that I may safely perform the journey and Mrs Spurgeon also: 'A thousand miles' is a serious word for such feeble folk. 'The Lord will perfect that which concerneth me,' and when I return to you in peace we will hold a public thanksgiving, and bless our healing Lord.

   I shall leave you in the hands of our God. As a church of the living God you are as 'a city set on a hill which cannot be hid'. Your love and unity, and prayer, and faith are known everywhere: will these bear the further strain which will be put upon them by the absence and feebleness of the Pastor? I believe they will: but let each one see to it that the part of service with which he or she may be individually concerned is carried on with more than past efficiency. Souls must be saved, and Jesus glorified whether the usual leader is present, or another, or no leader at all. The Lord hear my prayer for you, even as he has heard yours for me. I am far too feeble to make any public appearance, or I would come and plead that now in the hour of your testing you may be found as pure gold which fears not the continuance of the heat.

I beg your cooperation with my brother, and Mr Stott, and the officers in all the regular work and service of our Lord. I have called Dr Pierson from America with the view of an advance all along the line. I was bearing the cause on my heart, and thinking that as you had heard so many different men it might be well if, before my return, some one would be with you for a season – the same preacher for a time. No one suggested Dr Pierson to me: it came from my heart, and I think I was led of the Lord. This beloved brother is the author of several powerful works on the side of the truth, and a man of burning missionary zeal. I have had the closest fellowship of heart with him as a champion of the faith. Long ago he said to me that he would give up every occupation to serve me, ➤

Dr A. T. Pierson from Philadelphia ministered at the Tabernacle throughout this last illness and stayed on for the period after Spurgeon's death. He wrote back to his US magazine: 'This Metropolitan Tabernacle is a house of prayer most emphatically...prayer is almost ceaselessly going up. When one meeting is not in progress, another is. This is a hive of bees, where there are comparatively few drones. There are prayer meetings before preaching, and others after preaching...No marvel that Mr Spurgeon's ministry has been so blessed. He himself attributes it mainly to the prevailing prayers of his people. Why may not the whole Church of God learn something from the Metropolitan Tabernacle of London as to the power of simple gospel preaching backed by believing supplication? Referring to this great church, one cannot forget also its divine mission as a standing protest against the secularising of the house of God by the attractions of worldly art and aestheticism. Here is nothing to divert the mind from the simplicity of worship and the gospel...This lesson has, in my opinion, a bearing on all work for Christ, at home and abroad. Our reliance is too much on the charms of this world, in drawing souls to the gospel and to the Saviour. The Holy Spirit will not tolerate our idols. If we will have artistic and secular type of music, substituting unsanctified art for simple praise; if we will have elaborate ritual in place of simple, believing prayer; if we will have eloquent lectures in place of simple earnest gospel preaching, we must not wonder if no shekinah fires burn in our sanctuaries...Perhaps the reason why the work of God abroad shows more signs of his presence and power than our sanctuary services at home is in part this, that our foreign mission work has never been embarrassed as yet by those elaborate attempts at aesthetic attraction which turn many of our home churches into concert-halls and lecture-saloons and costly club-houses.'

➤ and I believed him. I sat down and wrote him; but the remarkable fact is that he had already written me so that the next day I heard from him, hinting that a time had come when his former offer might be renewed. I believe it is of the Lord. I am responsible for the action, and I look not for blame, but for the manifest approval of my Lord.

Let nothing flag. There may be some deficiencies to be made up on my return, but let these be as light as possible. If friends took their seats there would be none.

I am not going to burden myself with any care. I leave the flock with the Great Shepherd of the sheep, and feel that you will be both led and fed. The Lord grant that whether I speak or am silent, rejoice or suffer, live or die, all may be to his glory and the progress of his gospel. I am a debtor now to all the churches and to all classes of society. The sympathy shown me every day almost breaks my heart with gratitude. What am I?

One thing I know: I am your loving servant in Christ Jesus, and the Lord's messenger to many souls, who never saw me, but who have read the sermons. To you at Tabernacle I am very near of kin. God bless you.

Yours in our One Head

C. H. Spurgeon

(Portion of original)

Westwood, Beulah Hill, Upper Norwood
25th October 1891

Dear Friends,

Join with me in returning thanks for the measure of recovery with which our God has blessed me. I am not yet my former self. As to strength and as to the wasting disease which still remains I have a great deal of repair to desire: but all is hopeful. In due time, by God's good hand, I shall return to you much the same as when the hand of affliction set me on one side.

I am abashed at having written you so much about myself in all my former letters. Let me now speak of our Lord. His lovingkindness is exceeding great. The loving help and sympathy of friends is but a stream from that overflowing source. What can we render to him? I must answer this question in my own way; but I beg my dear church and people to give a glorious reply, such as may be expected of them.

Dr Pierson has come among you in humble but unwavering faith that the Lord is about to make bare his arm in our midst. The church officers saw this at their first meeting with him, and I want every member of the church to see the same. I hope he has come to reap where others of us have sown; and also to gather in some who had been withering by the wayside and were not in the field at all.

I expect a great revival. I pray for it and I look for it. If all remain lovingly united and hopefully active it will be so. Let those who are not workers for the Lord get to the service at once; and let veteran workers try to do more.

I pray that the services of this day both morning, afternoon, and evening may be as when the sun ariseth, a morning without clouds. May school, and college, and orphanage, and colportage, and all the varied works – start afresh.

Today pray for the Sabbath School specially, tomorrow come to ➤

➢ the prayer meeting and make it a sort of initial letter on a new page. If the Lord will bless you thus it will be his kindest way of blessing me. I live if you prosper. I could not rest even in the land where spring abides, if I saw you failing, or falling into divisions, or slack in prayer. You are my joy and crown, and at the same time my burden and care. God himself bless you.

Very gently I would say to you as to church matters. This year is a time of strain financially and it would rejoice me much if without any solicitation each steward of the Lord would make it his or her business to see that nothing is lacking for church needs.

Care for the poor, seek out the fallen, visit your fellow members when sick, by mingled prayer and thanks live near to God; and may the Lord bless you and your children both now and to eternity.

Yours in love most spiritual and abiding

C. H. Spurgeon

For myself, and my dear wife, and my brother and his wife, and Mr Harrald, please ask journeying mercies. You shall know how it speeds with us.

Mrs Spurgeon would later write of this period: 'The Lord so tenderly granted to us both three months of perfect earthly happiness here in Menton, before he took him to the "far better" of his own glory and immediate presence! For fifteen years my beloved had longed to bring me here; but it had never before been possible…We took long daily drives, and every place we visited was a triumphal entry for him. His enjoyment was intense, his delight exuberant. He looked in perfect health, and rejoiced in the brightest of spirits. Then, too, with what calm, deep happiness he sat, day after day, in a cosy corner of his sunny room, writing his last labour of love, the commentary on *Matthew's Gospel*…Up to the last ten days of his sweet life, health appeared to be returning, though slowly; our hopes were strong for his full recovery, and he himself believed that he should live to declare again to his dear people, and to poor sinners "the unsearchable riches of Christ".'

Terminus Hotel, Marseille
28th October 1891

My Dear Friends,

If I do not write to you today, which is only Wednesday, I could not get a letter to you for Sunday. This might be no loss to you; but it would be a trouble to me, for somehow it has grown to be a pleasing habit to keep in touch with you by a weekly letter.

Please praise the Lord for me and with me. I feel none the worse for the long journey I have already taken, but I am strangely better. All the story of my cure has been marvellous, and this last part of it is all a piece with the rest. 'He restoreth my soul', and 'he healeth all my diseases'. Let the name of the Lord be magnified, who has such compassion upon one who feels his own unworthiness more than ever. 'I was brought low, and he helped me.'

My doctor has reported my case to my friend, Dr FitzHenry, of Menton, who is a man of equal skill and kindness, – a happy blend; so that none of you may think that I am distant from medical help if any return of disease should come. But I do not anticipate further relapses, for the temperature even here is like that of summer, and further on we look for much more warmth: this will greatly diminish liability to chills.

But my one great restorative will be news of revival at the Tabernacle. When sinners are saved and saints are sanctified, my sun will have risen with healing in his wings. If the Lord will work by Dr Pierson, and Mr Stott, and the brethren at home, and make them useful at a tenfold rate compared with me in my best days, I will unfeignedly rejoice. 'Would God that all the Lord's people were prophets!' Oh, that he would use every man and woman of you! Those whom the Lord does not use are very apt to be seized by another, and turned to his evil purposes. Those who are not working ➤

➤ bees usually turn into dead flies, and spoil the sweetest ointments by the pot-full at a time. May no one in our church sink into such a wretched condition; far rather may we be so blest as to become blessings to all around!

Brethren and sisters, can you rise to a great opportunity? I think you can and will.

My beloved brother from America has not been sent into your midst for a small purpose. If you knew the whole story of how he came to be where he now is, you would feel this as strongly as I do. He brings the divine proffer of a great blessing; are we ready to receive it? Are we prepared to use a flood-tide? Oh, that every member may say 'I am'! Then ask what you will, believe that you have it, and go forth to ingather it. God never disappoints. We often lock doors against ourselves, and refuse to be enriched: let us do so no more – not one of us. Let us glorify God by accepting what he is waiting to bestow.

Accept each one my true love in Christ Jesus. Love one another with a pure heart fervently. My brother, whose care has made the journey less formidable, when he returns, will have a cheering tale to tell of me, and of my dear wife, whose presence with me makes every single enjoyment into seven. I am surrounded with unexpected mercies, and would ask you to help me to express a praise which one mouth can never adequately utter.

Yours most heartily

C. H. Spurgeon

(Portion of original)

Menton
31st October 1891

Beloved Friends,

I was supremely thankful to telegraph to London that I was not wearied by my journey of a thousand miles, but rather refreshed by it. I wrote that this was 'almost miraculous', and my dear brother observed that I might wisely leave out the 'almost', and so save twopence which is the rate per word. Well, it does seem to me to be beyond all that I could have asked or even thought. Blessed be the healing Lord!

I am waiting and watching for news from home as remarkable in regard to a Tabernacle revival as these tidings from me about my restoration to health. I now look for great things in connection with Dr Pierson's labours, and those of all my friends at home. Good news has already reached me as to the usefulness of the printed sermons; but I long for more. To spread my sermons is to help on the cause in the most efficient manner. To pray for a blessing is to share in it. Why should we not see a renewal of faith, a re-enthrone-ment of truth, a deep and wide-spread revival of religion at home, and a grand advance of missions abroad? According to your faith be it unto you; ye heirs of the heavenly kingdom!

Your fellow-servant

C. H. Spurgeon

(Portion of original from letter opposite)

Those who are not working bees usually turn into dead flies, to spoil the sweetest ointment of the pot-full at a time. May no one in our church sink into such a wretched condition; far rather may we be so blest as to become blessings to all around!

Menton
Thursday 5th November 1891

To The Tabernacle
Beloved Friends,

To reach you on the Lord's Day I write on Thursday. You wish to know how I am, and I will despatch the weary question in a few words. I am much the same as when I left home. Full of confidence that in answer to prayer I shall be perfectly restored, I must wait patiently in weakness till our heavenly Father gives me back my strength. It is no small trial to feel the desire to do many things, and yet to have to feel anew your inability in the simplest efforts. To go up a few steps, to take a short walk, to move a parcel, – and all such trifles, becomes a difficulty, so that Solomon's words are true 'the grasshopper is a burden'. I think I could preach, but when I have seen a friend for five minutes I begin to feel that I have had as much of speaking as I can well manage. Thus you see where I am, and while you thank God for his goodness in so far restoring me I again ask for your prayers that my disease may continue to decrease, and above all that I may have no relapse.

Far better is my other subject. From all I hear there is a hopeful interest excited in the ministry which the Lord has provided for you. The fish are round the boat. Now may the Lord enable the fisherman to cast the net skilfully, and may there be a great haul of great fishes. At times the greatest demand of the angler is for a landing net. He has a hold of the fish, but needs help in drawing him to shore. May every member of the church be such a landing net to the honoured preacher whom they hear. Some of you know the sacred art by long practice; let others commence the blessed habit. Souls are being awakened all around you. Beloved be awake yourselves. 'When thou hearest the sound of a going in the tops of the mulberry trees, then shalt thou bestir thyself.'

I am writing in the early morning of a warm day of brilliant sunshine; and the very thought of your holy assembly and your loving thoughts of me makes all this tenfold more powerful to cheer and to restore me. If I had not such an attached people I should miss my greatest earthly joy and succumb to the depression which physical weakness is so apt to produce. My dear brother will soon be with you to report of my behaviour, but I am doubly happy in having my beloved wife as my watchful companion, – a joy specially given in this peculiar hour of need.

The Lord himself bless every one of you, and specially those who minister in Word and doctrine.

Your loving friend

C. H. Spurgeon

The Pastors' College
Very early in his ministry, Spurgeon commenced the Pastors' College to train men in preaching and pastoral duties. Calvinistic theology was clearly taught and the men were infused with strong evangelistic zeal. It was an intensely practical two-year course with no degrees awarded, the key being that the students were part of the Tabernacle and gained a wealth of experience as they engaged in all the labours and teaching. Spurgeon's famous *Lectures to My Students* arose from his Friday afternoon addresses to them. He kept a close interest in the students and their work long after they had moved on to pastor churches. There were evening classes for those in employment, attended by hundreds of Tabernacle members, which also gave a basic secular education to those who had received limited schooling.

Menton
12th November 1891

Beloved Friends,

I have no striking progress to report, but I feel I must be better, whatever the signs may say. Still, feelings are doubtful evidences; and one thing is daily forced upon my mind, namely, that I am weak as water, and that building up is slower work than falling down.

Meanwhile, patience must have her perfect work, and I may well be quieted into cheerful submission because I receive such happy accounts of the blessing resting upon the labours of my dear friend, Dr Pierson. If nothing is injured by my absence, the trial of being away is not burdensome. If the Lord will bless my substitute more than he has done myself, I shall rejoice to have been put aside for a while. Now, in this matter, much depends upon each member personally. The Lord will bless you through yourselves. The missionary spirit burns in the heart of Dr Pierson, Mr Stott seems to be always on fire, others among your officers are zealots for souls, – may the whole mass be alight with heavenly fire! Then shall we see the congregation and the surrounding neighbourhood warmed with interest in the gospel, and at last melted into repentance by the heat of divine grace.

I am much at ease about the testimony of my pulpit, for our friend Dr Pierson does not flinch from defending truth and assailing false doctrine. From all I can hear, I judge that error is as rampant as ever, and is as much countenanced by the association of good men with those who hold it. If I had not borne my protest before, I should have been driven to bear it now. 'Evil men and seducers will wax worse and worse.' As for us, beloved, let us abide in that which the Holy Ghost has taught us, and may that which he has written in the Book be also written by his own hand upon all our hearts! The Lord, himself, bless you!

Yours with all my heart
C. H. Spurgeon

Menton
10th December 1891

Beloved Friends,

Every message from home concerning the work at the Tabernacle comforts me. Your unity of heart, and prayerfulness of spirit, are a joy to me. How much I wish that I could look you in the face, and lead you in prayer to the throne of the heavenly grace.

I am, however, glad that I am not yet standing on the platform among you attempting public prayer or address, for emotion would carry me away, and I should soon be quite exhausted. I put this to practical proof by offering prayer with some six or seven friends: I was overcome and was some time before I could recover myself. Still the mind is ready, and the physical frame must in due time follow the road to restoration: indeed I feel better, and have no fear but in due season I shall be as strong as aforetime.

It is not in my power to hasten to strength: this must come by degrees as the Lord may please to grant it. Pray for me that the time be not too long.

I want all those who take an interest in Tabernacle work to see that the funds are all right at the close of the year. My absence has tried the home cause very much, and I hope that every one will resolve that no deficiency shall occur in anything, for that would be a great grief to me. Be thoughtfully generous just now and it will be most seasonable. We must never allow home funds to be straitened, while we personally receive so freely of the grace of God.

Mrs Spurgeon and myself are happy to be privileged to be together in this sunny land; we are both of us full of gratitude that we are spared to each other, and both thankful to you for remembering us in your prayers.

God bless you each one
Yours ever heartily
C. H. Spurgeon

Menton

17th December 1891

My Dear Friends,

Though I cannot be present to wish you the blessings of the season, I would not use the words of compliments, but I would say from my heart, 'I wish you a most happy Christmas.' Upon your family gatherings may the best blessing rest! May all your children be the Lord's children, and thus may your union in the bonds of the flesh be made eternal by the bonds of the spirit! Joy be with you: yet let it be joy in the Lord.

I would beg you to remember my orphan charge, and make them merry on the day of the feast. Remember also the poor, and let no one lack if you are able to relieve, or to help in doing so.

I think I can fairly say, – I am better. Whether or no the disease is disappearing, I cannot say, though I fear there is not much difference; but in general health I must be improved, or else my feelings are sheer delusion. At any rate, I am very hopeful, and praiseful, and I wish I could stand up, and give out Psalm CIII.

The blessing of the Father, the Son, and the Holy Ghost be with each one of you, evermore!

Yours most heartily

C. H. Spurgeon

(Portion of original)

I am very hopeful, and praiseful, & I wish I could stand up, & give out Psalm CIII.

Menton

24th December 1891

My Dear Friends,

For the last time in the year 1891 I write you, and with this brief note I send hearty gratitude for your loving-kindness to me during the year which is ending, and fervent wishes for a special blessing on the year so soon to begin. I have nearly finished thirty-eight years of my ministry among you, and have completed XXXVII volumes of published sermons, preached in your midst. Yet we are not wearied of each other. I shall hail the day when I may again speak with you. Surrounded by ten thousand mercies, my time of weakness is rendered restful and happy; but still to be able, in health and vigour, to pursue the blissful path of useful service, would be my heaven below. To be denied activities which have become part of my nature, seems so strange; but as I cannot alter it, and as I am sure that infinite wisdom rules it, I bow before the divine will, – my Father's will.

Again the doctor reports favourably. That is to say, yesterday he said that there was decided improvement as to the disease: nothing great, but as much as he could hope for; – nothing speedy could be looked for, but matters were going most encouragingly. I was to be very careful about a chill, etc.

This is an old and dull story to you. Only your prayerful and persevering interest in me could make me bold enough to repeat it.

Honestly, I do not think you are losers by my absence, so long as the Lord enables our dear friend Dr Pierson to preach as he does. There is a cloud of blessing resting on you now. Turn the cloud into a shower by the heavenly electricity of believing prayer. May the watch-night be a night to be remembered, and on the first hour of the year may the Lord say 'From this day will I bless you.'

Yours with faithful love

C. H. Spurgeon

Menton
31st December 1891

My Dear Friends,

I am sorry my letter of last week reached London too late for reading on Sunday, but this was occasioned by delays in the trains, and
not by any omission on my part. It is kind on the part of so many
newspapers to publish it, for thus I trust most of you have read it.

I believe I am right in reporting a greater change in the disease
than could be spoken of before. It is still a great drain upon me; but
as it has improved so far, I believe it will make more rapid diminu-
tion. What a joy it will be to be within measurable distance of the
time to return to my pulpit and to you. I have not reached that point
yet.

Now may the Lord cause the cloud of blessing to burst upon you in
a great tropical shower. I am expecting this. Grateful beyond expression for all that the Lord has done and is doing, I am eager for more.
Indulgence in covetousness is sinful, but not when we 'covet earnestly
the best gifts'. All that I can do is to pray and expect. I am sometimes fearful lest anything in me should hinder the blessing; do you
not each one feel the same fear on your own account? Before some
sweet music is about to be heard there is a hush. Each one is afraid to
breathe lest the tone should be spoiled and the music marred. I feel
just so at this moment. May no whisper that would grieve the Holy
Spirit be heard in house or heart. Let all coldness, worldliness, difference, or selfishness be put forth as the old leaven, that we may keep

On the evening of 31st December 1891 and the morning of 1st January
1892, Spurgeon gave a short talk to a group of friends gathered in his
sitting-room. These two addresses are provided on pages 124-134.

He also wrote at this time the preface to the 1891 annual volume of
The Sword and the Trowel with comments on the lessons to be learned
from his illness. This is shown on page 122.

the feast of New Year without anything that defileth.

The Lord himself deal out to each one of his children a full portion, and to those who linger at the gate may the Good Spirit give his gracious drawings that they may cross the sacred threshold this day. Peace be within the gates of our dear sanctuary, and prosperity within her doors. For my brethren and companions sake will I now say 'peace be within thee.'

Yours to serve when I can and to love unceasingly

C. H. Spurgeon

A portrait of Spurgeon on his
last day of reasonable health.

Menton
6th January 1892

My Dear Friends,

There is nothing for me to say in reporting myself to head-quarters beyond this – that I hope and believe that the steady and solid progress which had begun is continued, and will continue. If a doctor were to visit me now for the first time, and were to investigate my disease, he would pronounce it a bad case. But those who know what I have been, and how much worse than at present everything was – must wonder at me, and think it is a remarkably good case. God be thanked for all that he has done in answer to his people's prayers. Never let us have a doubt as to the fidelity and ability of the God of the promises and of the mercy-seat.

On looking back upon the valley of the shadow of death through which I passed so short a time ago, I feel my mind grasping with firmer grip than ever that everlasting gospel which for so many years I have preached to you. We have not been deceived. Jesus does give rest to those who come to him, he does save those who trust him, he does photograph his image on those who learn of him. I hate the Christianised infidelity of the modern school more than ever, as I see

On 9th January Spurgeon completed the last revision of a sermon manuscript: *Psalm 105.37* – 'A Stanza of Deliverance'. On 13th January he wrote a note for the February 1892 issue of *The Sword and the Trowel* on the Bible and Modern Criticism:–

'By this time we shall scarcely again be charged with wantonly raising the cry of "Wolf" without a cause, when we earnestly warned the churches that infidelity was permeating the ministry. A fierce controversy is now raging, everywhere, over the inspiration of the Holy Scriptures; and this is involving the Deity of our Lord, and indeed every other truth of Christianity.'

After an account of the current events he concluded:–

'To be free from all ecclesiastical entanglements is to the Christian minister a blessing worth all it has cost, even though an almost fatal illness might be reckoned as part of the price.'

how it rends away from sinful man his last and only hope. Cling to the gospel of forgiveness through the substitutionary sacrifice, and spread it with all your might, each one of you, for it is the only cure for bleeding hearts.

Peace be unto you as a whole; and peace be to each one! I greet with whole-hearted gratitude my brother Dr Pierson, and with unfeigned love each deacon, elder, and member, and worker. My own dear brother in the flesh is also ever watching over the concerns of our great work. May the Lord himself keep watch over all. To Mr Stott I wish a long and prosperous ministry where the Lord shall direct him.

Yours ever lovingly

C. H. Spurgeon

The funeral procession entering Norwood Cemetery
(from the *Daily Graphic* of 20th February 1892). See page 121 for details.

Menton
14th January 1892

My Dear Friends,

I have not seen the doctor since writing last time, and I have therefore little to say about my health so far as medical testimony goes. We have had a week of broken, uncertain weather; days of rain, intervals of wind, and hours of cold. This has kept me very much within doors, for I dare not run the risk of a chill; and therefore I fear I have made no progress, and can hardly hope that I am quite so well, as to my internal mischief. In other respects I feel fairly up to the mark, and deeply grateful to be free from pain, and free from fear as to the ultimate result.

I earnestly hope that your weather will improve. When it is bad here what must it be with you. The snow on the mountains reminds us of what others are enduring. I wish I could be in such health as to be always with you, but as this cannot be I am most thankful for the retreat afforded by this sheltered spot, and even more so for the rest of heart which comes to me through knowing that you are all spiritually fed under the ministry of Dr Pierson. May his health be maintained and that of his wife during your trying winter.

You may feel sure that I am doing pretty well, or the doctor would be looking me up. When he next calls I will have a bulletin from him; and till then you may rest in peace about me. May the saturating showers of blessing, for which I am looking, soon fall in tropical abundance, and may no part of the field be left dry. If there are any very sad, downcast, and self-condemned ones among you, I desire my special love to them. The Lord himself looks from Heaven to spy out such special characters. See Job XXXIII.27, 28. I think this text is a message for somebody. May grace abound towards you.

Yours ever heartily
C. H. Spurgeon

On 20th January, Spurgeon went for his last drive in Menton. In the evening he suffered from pain in the hand, and in the morning severe head pain, which, he said, ached just as it did at the start of his serious illness in the summer. Spurgeon now made several significant remarks to his secretary Harrald, such as: 'My work is done', indicating he knew that his end was approaching. During the following days he was mainly unconscious, until dying on 31st January. His widow prayed with the small company with her, thanking the Lord for the precious treasure so long lent her, and asking for strength and help. She was later to telegraph to 'Son Tom' – 'Father in Heaven. Mother resigned.'

Right: the telegram sent by Harrald from Menton to the church officers.

More than a thousand police officers were supplied along the four-mile route of the funeral procession to Norwood Cemetery (below). Spurgeon had said eighteen years before – 'When you see my coffin carried to the silent grave, I should like every one of you, whether converted or not, to be constrained to say, "He did earnestly urge us, in plain and simple language, not to put off the consideration of eternal things. He did entreat us to look to Christ."'

Preface to Spurgeon's Last Annual
Volume of *The Sword and the Trowel*
written at the end of 1891

OUR MINISTRY at the Tabernacle has been sorrowfully brief during 1891. It opened happily enough, with congregations undiminished, and converts coming forward in large numbers; and then the clouds descended, and the customary voice was hushed. Yet, possibly; nay, we may say, assuredly, the Lord has done greater things by his servant's sickness and silence than by his health and verbal testimony. We may not always expect to see the why and wherefore of the Lord's dealings; but, in this case, certain points are clear enough.

The work which centres at the Metropolitan Tabernacle has been tested. It has been assumed by many that the death of the pastor would be fatal to the work which he has inaugurated. This has been shown to be a mere assumption. Like Isaac, he was 'as good as dead', but the institutions were maintained, and the preaching of the Word was sustained by divers men of God, till at last the man came [A. T. Pierson] who has filled the great house, and moved the heart of the crowd by his noble witness for the truth. The members have not forsaken the church, and the workers have not stayed their hand. Such an experience is reassuring, and is a practical rehearsal of what will surely be done on another day, when he, who has again and again been drawn out of the waters of death, shall in very deed go up the mount, and fall asleep, and no more lead the flock through the wilderness.

Very notable is the fact that an immense amount of fervent prayer has been drawn forth. On no modern occasion known to us has more supplication been made to God for the life of a minister of the gospel. Of course, our own dear people were constant and instant in their pleadings; but this was only as the drop of a bucket compared with the intercessions of millions all over the world. There is no exaggeration in this estimate; it really seemed as if all bodies of Christians, and even others beyond the pale of our holy faith, were at one in crying to God on our behalf. Had the prayers remained unanswered, great occasion to blaspheme would have been taken by the enemy. As it is, the fact has greatly aided faith in candid minds. The preservation of a life so nearly gone was, if we may not say 'miraculous', at least a very remarkable instance of the prevalence of united prayer in a desperate case. The lesson thus taught by public fact cannot be lost on thoughtful minds. Several pastors have stated that their people had allowed the prayer meeting to droop; but when invited to pray in this case, they came together in numbers, and pleaded fervently for the special object, and have continued in the fuller exercise of prayer ever since. It is worthwhile to be sore sick if thereby men are cured of the sorer sickness of neglect of prayer.

Equally memorable is the latent Christian love which has been made manifest. Spontaneously, loving telegrams and letters poured in, not from well-known friends only, but more numerously from persons of other denominations, from whom tender sympathy and concern might not have been expected...

Strength and space alike fail the Editor, and he patiently resumes the couch, to which he is bound to return by the careful reminders of those who watch over him. Gratitude, to God and to all sorts of friends, brings the water into his eyes as he writes. Blessed be the Lord, who healeth us, and blessed be the hearts that implored his gracious interposition, and blessed be every reader of these pages!

So prays

C. H. Spurgeon

Spurgeon's Last Close-of-Year Message, given at Menton

on the last evening of 1891
(Edited from *The Sword and the Trowel,* February, 1892)

Dear Friends,

I am not able to say much to you at present. I should have gladly invited you to prayer every morning if I had been able to meet you; but I had not sufficient strength. I cannot refrain from saying a little to you, on this the last evening of the year, by way of retrospect, and perhaps on new year's morning I may add a word by way of prospect.

We have come so far on the journey of life; and, standing at the boundary of another year, we look back. Let each one gaze upon his own trodden pathway. You will not need me to attempt fine words or phrases: each one, with his own eyes, will now survey his own road. Among the striking things to be noted are the dangers we have escaped. After Bunyan's pilgrim had safely traversed the Valley of the Shadow of Death, the morning light dawned upon him, and sitting down, he looked back upon the terrible road which he had passed. It had once seemed an awful thing to him that he had marched through that valley by night; but when he looked back, and saw the horrors he had escaped, he must have felt glad that darkness had concealed much of its peril when he was actually in the midst of it. Much the same has it been with us: thank God, now that we clearly see the perils, we have passed them in safety.

During the year which closes this night, certain of us have been very near to the jaws of death, and some of us may also have skirted the abyss of despair; and yet we live and hope. Our path has been full of trials and temptations, and yet we have not been permitted to fall. Our heart has been torn with inward conflicts, and yet faith has proved victorious. No one of us knows how near he has been to some great sin, or some false step.

Let us thank God for preserved lives, continued comforts, and unspotted characters; for these wares are marked 'Fragile', and that they are not broken is a marvel of grace.

Since last we met, how many have died! Plagues and deaths have been flying around us, like shots in the heat of an action; and only he who, of old, covered David's head in the day of battle, could have kept us from death. Our spiritual life still survives, and only he who holds the stars in their courses could have maintained us in our integrity. It ought to bring tears of gratitude to our eyes while, to quote the language of the *Song of Solomon*, we 'look from the top of Hermon, from the lions' dens, from the mountains of the leopards'.

For my own part, I dare not omit from my retrospect the sins of the past year, of which I would unfeignedly repent. He who does not know himself to be sinful does not know himself at all. He who does not feel his own unworthiness must surely have grown callous or conceited. Sins of omission are those which trouble me most. I look back, and remember what I might have done, and have not done; what opportunities of usefulness I have not seized; what sins I have allowed to pass unrebuked; what struggling beginners in grace I have failed to help. I cannot but grieve that what I have done was not done better, or attended with a humbler dependence upon God.

I now perceive, in my holy things, faults in their beginning, faults in their carrying on, and faults in their ending. Delay to commence, slackness in the act, and pride after it, defile our best service. What an endless list our faults and failings would make! Oh, friends, when we examine one year of life carefully, looking into the thoughts and motives and secret imaginings of the soul, how humbled we ought to be! As I rode through the streets of Menton this day, I felt bowed down with a sense of sin; and on a sudden it flashed into my mind, 'Yes, and therefore, I have my part and lot in the work of the Lord Jesus, for he said expressly, "I came not to call the righteous, but sinners."'

Why did Jesus die? He died for our sins: he would not have needed to die for men if men had not sinned. Where there is no sin, there is no share in the sin-offering. If we have no sin, we have no connection with that Saviour who came to save his people from their sins. For whom does Jesus plead? He makes intercession for the transgressors: if I am not a transgressor, I have no assurance that he pleads for me. The whole mediatorial system is for sinful men; and as I am conscious of guilt, so am I assured, by faith, that I am within the circle of divine grace.

My faith places her hand upon the head of him who was our Substitute and Scapegoat, and I see all my sins and all the sins of all believers for ever put away by him who stood in the sinner's place.

Let your tears fall because of sin; but, at the same time, let the eye of faith steadily behold the Son of man lifted up, as Moses lifted up the serpent in the wilderness, that those who are bitten by the old serpent may look unto him and live. Our sinnership is that emptiness into which the Lord pours his mercy. 'This is a faithful saying, and worthy of all acceptation, that Christ Jesus came into the world to save sinners.' On that blessed fact I rest my soul. Though I have preached Christ crucified for more than forty years, and have led many to my Master's feet, I have at this moment no ray of hope but that which comes from what my Lord Jesus has done for guilty men.

> *Behold him there! the bleeding Lamb!*
> *My perfect, spotless Righteousness,*
> *The great unchangeable, 'I AM',*
> *The King of glory and of grace.*

A flood of light breaks over the scene if we look back upon our mercies! Now for your arithmetic! Now begin to make your calculations! Think of major mercies and minor mercies; fleeting mercies and eternal mercies; mercies by day, and mercies by night; mercies averting evil, and mercies securing good; mercies at home, and mercies abroad; mercies of bed and board, of city and field, of society and seclusion. Mercy affects every faculty of the mind, and every portion of the body. There are mercies for conscience, and fear, and hope; mercies for the understanding and the heart; and, at the same time, there are mercies of eye, and ear, and head, and hand. The whole landscape of life is golden with the light of mercy. In the love of God we have lived, and moved, and had our being. We see mercies new every morning, mercies old as the eternal hills; streams of mercy; oceans of mercy; mercy all, and all mercy.

God has been specially good to me. I think I hear each heart whisper, 'That is just what I was going to say.' Dear friends, I will not monopolise the expression: it is most true for me; I doubt not that it is also true of each one of you. Can we conceive how God could have been more gracious than he has been? If you are familiar with the Lord of love, so that you dwell in him, and his Spirit dwells in you, you will join me in abundantly uttering the memory of his great goodness. How wonderful is his lovingkindness! How free! How tender! How faithful! How lasting! How everlasting! No, I cannot even attempt an outline of the Lord's goodness to us during the year which is now waning: we must each one review the record for himself. 'How much owest thou unto my Lord?' is an enquiry which must be personally answered by each one as an individual.

One thing more before I close. What are the lessons which our gracious God has intended us to learn by all that has happened during the year? Each one of us has had his own order of discipline and line of learning; but all have not had the same. It is written, 'All thy children shall be taught of the Lord,' but all the children are not reading from the same page, at the same moment.

Have we not learned to expect more of God, and less of men? To make fewer resolutions, but to carry out those which were wisely and devoutly formed? Have we not seen more of the instability of earthly joys? Have we not learned more fully the need of using time present, and ability possessed? Are we not now aware that we are neither so good, so wise, so strong, nor so constant as we thought we were? Have we been taught to go down that Jesus may rise, after the manner of John the Baptist, who cried, 'He must increase, but I must decrease'?

These are truths worth learning. I have neither time nor strength to suggest more of those lessons which experience teaches us when our hearts are made ready for the divine schooling. We ought to have learned much in 365 days. I hope we have. Permit me only to hint at a truth which has come home to me.

During the past year I have been made to see that there is more love and unity among God's people than is generally believed. I speak not egotistically, but gratefully. I had no idea that Christian people, of every church, would spontaneously and importunately plead for the prolonging of my life. I feel myself a debtor to all God's people on this earth. Each section of the church seemed to vie with all the rest in sending words of comfort to my wife, and in presenting intercession to God on my behalf.

If anyone had prophesied, twenty years ago, that a dissenting minister, and a very outspoken one too, would be prayed for in many parish churches, and in Westminster Abbey and St Paul's Cathedral, it would not have been believed; but it was so. There is more love in the hearts of Christian people than they know of themselves. We mistake our divergencies of judgement for differences of heart; but they are far from being the same thing. In these days of infidel criticism, believers of all sorts will be driven into sincere unity. For my part, I believe that all spiritual persons are already one.

When our Lord prayed that his church might be one, his prayer was answered, and his true people are even now, in spirit and in truth, one in him. Between rationalism and faith there is an abyss immeasurable; but where there is faith in the Everlasting Father, faith in the Great Sacrifice, and faith in the Indwelling Spirit, there is a living, loving, lasting union.

I have learned, also, that when the one church pleads with hearty entreaties, she must and will be heard. No case is hopeless when many pray. The deadliest diseases relax their hold before the power of unanimous intercession. As long as I live, I am a visible embodiment of the fact that, to the prayer of faith, presented by the Church of God, nothing is impossible. It is worthwhile to have been sore sick to have learned this truth, and to have proved it in one's own person.

In this little circle, probably one and another may say, 'These are not exactly the lessons that we have learned this year.' Perhaps not. But if you have learned more of Jesus, and of his love, which passes knowledge, it suffices. Be thankful if you have learned even a little of Jesus. Do not judge yourself by the attainments of others who are older or more experienced; but rejoice in the Lord. Bless God for starlight, and he will give you moonlight; praise him for moonlight, and he will give you sunlight; thank him for sunlight, and you shall yet come to that land where they need not the light of the sun, for the Lord God giveth them light for ever and ever. May this year close with blessing! Amen.

Spurgeon's Last Opening-of-Year Message, given at Menton
on the first day of 1892
(Edited from *The Sword and the Trowel,* February, 1892)

Dear Friends,

Passing at this hour over the threshold of the new year, we look forward, and what do we see? Could we procure a telescope which would enable us to see to the end of the year, should we be wise to use it? I think not. We know nothing of the events which lie before us: of life or death to ourselves or to our friends, or of changes of position, or of sickness or health. What a mercy that these things are hidden from us!

If we foresaw our best blessings, they would lose their freshness and sweetness while we impatiently waited for them. Anticipation would sour into weariness, and familiarity would breed contempt. If we could foresee our troubles, we should worry ourselves about them long before they came, and in that fretfulness we should miss the joy of our present blessings. Great mercy has hung up a veil between us and the future; and there let it hang.

Still, all is not concealed. Some things we clearly see. I say, 'we'; but I mean those whose eyes have been opened, for it is not everyone who can see in the truest sense. A lady said to Mr Turner, 'I have often looked upon that prospect, but I have never seen what you have put into your picture.' The great artist simply replied, 'Don't you wish you could see it?' Looking into the future with the eye of faith, believers can see much that is hidden from those who have no faith. Let me tell you, in a few words, what I see as I look into the new year.

I see a pathway made from this first of January, 1892, to the first of January, 1893. I see a highway cast up by the foreknowledge and predestination of God. Nothing of the future is left to chance; nay, not the falling of a sparrow, nor the losing of a hair is left to haphazard; but all the events of life are arranged and appointed. Not only is every turn in the road marked in the divine map, but every stone on the road, and every drop of morning dew or evening mist that falls upon the grass which grows at the roadside. We are not to cross a trackless desert; the Lord has ordained our path in his infallible wisdom and infinite love. 'The steps of a good man are ordered by the Lord: and he delighteth in his way.'

I see, next, a Guide provided, as our companion along the way. To him we gladly say, 'Thou shalt guide me with thy counsel.' He is waiting to go with us through every portion of the road. 'The Lord, he it is that doth go before thee; he will be with thee, he will not fail thee.' We are not left to pass through life as though it were a lone wilderness, a place of dragons and owls; for Jesus says, 'I will not leave you comfortless: I will come to you.'

Though we should lose father, and mother, and the dearest friends, there is One who wears our nature, who will never quit our side. One like unto the Son of man is still treading the life-ways of believing hearts, and each true believer cometh up from the wilderness, leaning upon the Beloved. We feel the presence of the Lord Jesus even now, in this room, where two or three are gathered in his name; and I trust we shall feel it through all the months of the year, whether it be the time of the singing of birds, or the season of ripe fruits, or the dark months when the clods are frozen into iron.

In this Riviera, we ought the more readily to realise our Lord's presence, because the country is so like 'thy land, O Immanuel!' Here is the land of olive oil, and of figs, and of the clusters of Eshcol. By such a blue sea he walked, and up such rocky hills he climbed. But whether here, or elsewhere, let us look for HIM to abide with us, to make this year truly to be 'a year of our Lord'.

Beside the way and the Guide, I perceive very clearly, by the eye of faith, strength for the journey provided. Throughout the whole distance of the year, we shall find halting-places, where we may rest and take refreshment, and then go on our way singing, 'He restoreth my soul.' We shall have strength enough, but none to spare; and that strength will come when it is needed, and not before. When saints imagine that they have strength to spare, they turn sinners, and are apt to have their locks shorn by the Philistines. The Lord of the way will supply the pilgrims with sufficient spending-money for the road; but he may not think it wise to burden them with superfluous funds.

God all-sufficient will not fail those who trust him. When we come to the place for shouldering the burden, we shall reach the place for receiving the strength. If it pleases the Lord to multiply our troubles from one to ten, he will increase our strength in the same proportion. To each believer the Lord still says, 'As thy days, so shall thy strength be.' You do not yet feel that you have grace to die with: what of that? You are not yet dying. While you have yet to deal with the business and duty of life, look to God for the grace which these require; and when life is ebbing out, and your only thought is about landing on the eternal shore, then look to God your Saviour for dying grace in dying moments.

We may expect an inrush of divine strength when human strength is failing, and a daily impartation of energy as daily need requires. Our lamps shall be trimmed as long as they shall need to burn. Let not our present weakness tempt us to limit the Holy One of Israel. There is a hospice on every pass over the Alps of life, and a bridge across every river of trial which crosses our way to the Celestial City. Holy angels are as numerous to guard us as fallen ones to tempt us. We shall never have a need for which our gracious Father has furnished no supply.

I see, most plainly, a power overruling all things which occur in the way we tread. I see an alembic in which all things are transformed. 'All things work together for good to them that love God, to them who are the called according to his purpose.' I see a wonder-working hand which turns for us the swords of disease into the plough-shares of correction, and the spears of trial into the pruning-hooks of discipline. By this divine skill, bitters are made sweet, and poisons turned to medicines. 'Nothing shall by any means hurt you,' is a promise too strong for feeble faith; but full assurance finds it true. Since God is for us, who can be against us? What a joy to see Jehovah himself as our banner, and God himself with us as our Captain! Forward then into the new year, 'for there shall no evil befall thee.'

One thing more, and this is brightness itself: this year we trust we shall see God glorified by us and in us. If we realise our chief end, we reach our highest enjoyment. It is the delight of the renewed heart to think that God can get glory out of such poor creatures as we are. 'God is light.' We cannot add to his brightness; but we may act as reflectors, which, though they have no light of their own, yet, when the sun shines upon them, reflect his beams, and send them where, without such reflection, they might not have come. When the Lord shines upon us, we will cast that light upon dark places, and make those who sit in the shadow of death to rejoice in Jesus our Lord.

We hope that God has been in some measure glorified in some of us during the past year, but we trust he will be glorified by us far more in the year which now begins. We will be content to glorify God either actively or passively. We would have it so happen that, when our life's history is written, whoever reads it will not think of us as 'self-made men', but as the handiwork of God, in whom his grace is magnified. Not in us may men see the clay, but the Potter's hand. They said of one, 'He is a fine preacher;' but of another they said, 'We never notice how he preaches, but we feel that God is great.'

We wish our whole life to be a sacrifice; an altar of incense continually smoking with sweet perfume unto the Most High. Oh, to be borne through the year on the wings of praise to God; to mount from year to year, and raise at each ascent a loftier and yet lowlier song unto the God of our life! The vista of a praiseful life will never close, but continue throughout eternity. From psalm to psalm, from hallelujah to hallelujah, we will ascend the hill of the Lord; until we come into the holiest of all, where, with veiled faces, we will bow before the Divine Majesty in the bliss of endless adoration. Throughout this year may the Lord be with you! Amen.

The Seven Sneezes
by C. H. Spurgeon

**A short sermon written while ill at Menton in 1879,
providing strikingly rich counsel on how to help seekers.
(Edited)**

'The child sneezed seven times' *(2 Kings 4.35).*

THE CHILD WAS DEAD. Although he had been the special gift of divine promise and was therefore doubly prized by his parents, yet the little lad was not secure from the common hazards of life. He was in the harvest field in the heat of the day, when sunstroke smote him down. His father bade one of his young men carry him home, and he died on his mother's knees. The brave woman was heart-broken, but, being full of energy and spirit, she rode off to Elisha, the man of God, to tell him her sorrow, and to upbraid him with the short-lived blessing which had come to her through his prayers.

She clung to the prophet in the hour of her bitter sorrow, and he with his whole heart sympathised in her motherly grief. He hastened to the chamber where the dead child was laid upon the bed, and there, alone, he exercised the sacred power of prayer. Again and again he wrestled, and at length prevailed, so that in the glad Shunammite's case it was true that 'women received their dead raised to life again.' Such was the power of faith when it used the weapon of all prayer:

even the gates of the grave could not prevail against it.

The prophet's mode of operation when he lay upon the child and put his mouth upon the boy's mouth, 'and his eyes upon his eyes, and his hands upon his hands', is full of instruction. Spiritual life is the gift of God, but if the dead are to be raised by our means we must enter into hearty sympathy with them. We must create spiritual contact, and become in a great measure identified with those whom we would bless.

The Holy Ghost works by those who feel that they would lay down their own lives for the good of others, and would impart to them not only their goods and their instructions, but themselves also, if by any means they might save some. O for more Elishas, for then we should see more sinners raised from their death in sin.

The first clear evidence that the child was restored to life was his sneezing. Doubtless, it greatly rejoiced the prophet's heart. We, too, who are seeking the good of others will greatly exult if we are favoured to see gracious tokens in those for whose good we labour. At all gospel meetings earnest people should be on the look-out for persons convinced of sin, aroused in conscience or in any other manner made to feel the power of the life-giving Spirit. It will be well if these persons watch with instructed eyes, so that they do not overlook that which should give them full content.

Of natural life we may discern the tokens more readily than of spiritual life. We need practice and experience in reference to this more mysterious matter, or we may cause great pain to ourselves and to those whom we would befriend. We may gather instruction from the signs of life which contented the prophet: 'the child sneezed seven times.'

This evidence of life was very simple. Nothing is freer from art than a sneeze. It is so far from being artificial that it is involuntary. As a rule we sneeze, not because we will, but because we must. No instruction, education, talent, or acquirement is necessary to a sneeze, nor even to a series of seven sneezes; it is the act of a child, or of an illiterate peasant, quite as much as of a philosopher or a divine. Yet Elisha asked no further evidence of life. He did not require the little lad to repeat a psalm, or walk a mile, or climb a tree; he knew that he was alive although the act of the newly-given life was of the most elementary kind.

Just so let us feel thankful when we hear the first groan of distress or see the first tear of repentance. Hopefulness is a helpful element in the success of those who have to deal with seeking sinners. We ought not to expect too much in enquirers; we ought not to be satisfied without signs of life; but the faintest sign of life ought to encourage us and lead us to encourage them. Very little *knowledge* can be looked for in enquirers; Elisha did not ask the child to say his catechism. Very little *strength* will be found in them; Elisha did not bid the child move the table, and the stool, and the candlestick with which the room was furnished. No, the sneeze proved life, though it was inarticulate, and the uninstructed expression of untrained vitality.

Repentance for sin, desire after holiness, childlike trust in Jesus, tearful prayer, careful walking, delight in the Word of God, and intense self-distrust are among the elementary tokens of life, the sneezes of those freshly raised from the dead. Such tokens are to be seen in all the truly living in Zion, whether old or young, and hence they are not proofs of growth, but of life, and it is life that we have to deal with at the first; growth is a later consideration. Elisha did not leave the child upon the bed till he had developed into a man, but as soon as he had heard him sneeze he said to the mother, 'Take up thy son'; and we would earnestly say to every church in whose midst a soul has been born unto God, 'Take up thy son.' Receive the convert, though he be weak in the faith. Carry the lamb in thy bosom, cherish and nurture him till life has girded itself with manly strength.

This evidence of life was in itself unpleasant. To the child it was no pleasure to sneeze. We should most of us prefer to be excused from sneezing seven times. Many of the surest marks of the new life are by no means pleasurable. The regenerate are not at once happy; on the contrary, they are often in great bitterness for their sins, and in sore anguish because they have pierced their Saviour. The divine life is not born into the world without pangs. When a man has been nearly drowned, and animation is restored by rubbing, the first movements of the blood within the veins causes tingling and other sensations which are exquisitely painful. Sin causes numbness of soul, and this is attended by an absence of sensation; this is changed when life comes with its look of faith, for the first result is that men look on him whom they have pierced, and mourn for him. Some regard pleasurable emotions as the clearest signs of grace, but they are not so. 'I am so happy,' is frequently a far less certain token than 'I am so grieved because I have sinned.' We do not think much of the song of 'happy day', unless it has been preceded by the mournful ditty, 'O that my load of sin were gone!'

A sneeze is not very musical to those who hear it, and so the first signs of grace are not in themselves pleasing to those who are watching for souls. Our minds may be greatly pained to see the sorrow and despondency of the stricken heart, and yet that which we see may be nonetheless a certain sign of renewed life. We cannot take delight in heartbreak and convulsion of soul when considered in themselves; on the contrary, our earnest endeavour is to apply the balm of the gospel and remove such pains; yet are they among the most assured marks of the life of God in the soul in its earlier stages, and we ought to be thankful whenever we see them. That which worldlings condemn as melancholy is often to us a hopeful sign of thoughtfulness; and the self-despair which the ignorant deplore is cause for congratulation among those who pray for conversions. We delight in the sorrows of penitents because of their results, otherwise we take no delight in human grief, but the very reverse.

The evidences of life in the child were very monotonous. Again and again there came a sneeze and nothing else. No song, no note of music, not even one soft word, but sneeze, sneeze, sneeze, seven times. Yet the noises wearied not the prophet, who was far too glad to hear the sounds of life than to be particular about their musical character. The child lived, and that was enough for him. Much of the talk of enquirers is very wearisome; they tell the same melancholy tale over and over again. Answered a score times, they return to the same questions and repeat the same doubts. If one were seeking interest and variety, he would not look for it in the painful repetitions of persons under conviction of sin: though when we are watching for men's souls we do not grow weary, yet in themselves the utterances of the newly awakened are frequently among the most tiresome of communications. They are often difficult to understand, involved, confused, and even absurd; they frequently betray culpable ignorance and sinful obstinacy, combined with pride, unbelief, and self-will; and yet in them there is a secret something which betokens an awakening to the higher life; and therefore we cheerfully lend our ear.

After days of exhortation and consolation we find them still floundering in the slough of despond, sticking fast in the mire, out of which they seem half unwilling to be drawn. We find we must render them the same help over and over again, and point out the stepping stones for the hundredth time. Better that our service should be monotonous than that a soul should perish. The poor child may sneeze seven times if it will, and we will gladly hear it, for it is a joy thus to know that it lives; and our poor neighbour may repeat his painful story until seventy times seven, if therein we can discover traces of the work of the Spirit upon his soul.

Let us not be disappointed because at first we get little which is interesting from young converts. We are not examining for the ministry; we are only looking for evidences of spiritual life. To apply to them the tests which would be suitable for the testing of a doctor of divinity would be both cruel and ridiculous. In preachers of the gospel we expect variety, and wish we could have more of it, but from the babe in grace we are quite content to hear a cry, and a cry is not a subject for musical variations any more than a sneeze.

Yet the sound which entered the prophet's ear was a sure token of life, and we must not be content with any doubtful or merely hopeful signs. We want evidences of life, and these we must have. We long to see our friends really and truly saved and showing that they have passed from death unto life. We rejoice in the lowest form of that proof, but with less than this we cannot be quiet. Mere resolves to reform, or even reform itself, will not end our anxiety. No fine talk, or expressed emotion, or remarkable excitement will at all content us; we want them to be converted, to be born again from above, to be made new creatures in Christ Jesus.

The child might have been washed and dressed in his best clothes, but this would not have fulfilled the prophet's desire. The lad might have been decked with a chaplet of flowers, and his young cheeks might have been rouged into the imitation of a ruddy blush, but the holy man would have remained unsatisfied, for he must have a sign of life. However simple, it must assuredly be a life-token, or it would be in vain. Nothing could have been more conclusive than a sneeze.

We remember a case in which a loving watcher fancied that a corpse moved its arm, but it was only imagination supporting the wish of affection. However, there could be no room for a mistake in a sneeze, much less in seven sneezes. The prophet could safely call in the mother and commit to her care her undoubtedly living boy. So we also ask for indisputable marks of grace, and till we see them we shall still pray and watch and feel painful anxiety.

So far we have kept to the text, and as our space is limited we can only add these few precepts. Let Christians believe that their Lord can raise the spiritually dead. Let them make the ungodly their daily care. Let them bring them where souls are quickened – namely, under the sound of the gospel; and then let them prayerfully and wisely watch for results. The more watchers in a congregation the better; they will be the preacher's best allies, and greatly increase the fruit of his labours. What sayest thou, dear friend in Christ, can you not attempt this service? It requires graces rather than gifts, affection rather than talent. Rouse yourself to this delightful service, and watch until you see the signs of spiritual vitality. However unnoticed by others, let them not escape your eye, and ear and heart, but be ready to take care of the newly-quickened one, even if there be no more to be said of him than that 'the child sneezed seven times.'

Satan's Punctuality, Power, and Purpose
by C. H. Spurgeon

A short sermon written at Menton in 1879 encouraging constant prayer for the acceptance of the gospel word. (Edited)

'Then cometh the devil, and taketh away the word out of their hearts, lest they should believe and be saved' *(Luke 8.12)*.

THE THOUGHTS excited by the sight of a vast congregation are not all pleasurable; the question most naturally arises – What will come of all this preaching and hearing? Will the heavenly seed produce a harvest or fall on barren soil?

The anxious observer remembers that the arch-enemy of God and man is opposed to the salvation of souls and is present with destructive power wherever the seed of the Word is being sown. It is of this we shall now speak, – the activity of Satan during the preaching of the gospel. He is out of sight, but we may not allow him to be out of mind. He does all the more mischief if men sleep, so let us watchfully turn our eyes towards him and prove that we are not ignorant of his devices.

Our divine Lord in the words before us reminded his hearers of the devil's punctuality – 'then cometh the devil'; of his power – 'and taketh away the word out of their hearts'; and of his purpose, which is the prevention of saving faith – 'lest they should believe and be saved'. At this time, when special services are being held, it may be well to bring these points clearly forward that all may be warned against the wicked one, and so by the grace of God his designs may be frustrated.

I. First observe the evil one's PUNCTUALITY. No sooner does the seed fall than the fowls devour it. Our text says 'then,' which means – there and then, 'cometh the devil'. Mark renders it, 'Satan cometh immediately.' Whoever else may loiter, Satan never does. No sooner does a camel fall dead in the wilderness than the vultures appear. Not a bird was visible, nor did it seem possible that there could be one within a radius of many miles, yet speedily there are specks in the sky, and soon the devourers are gorging themselves with flesh. Even so do the spirits of evil scent their prey from afar, and hasten to their destroying work.

The lapse of time might give opportunity for thought, and thought might lead to repentance, and therefore the enemy hurries to prevent the hearer from considering the truth he has heard. When the gospel has somewhat affected the hearers, so that in some slight degree it is in their hearts, then swifter than the flight of the eagle is the hurry of the devil to take the Word out of their hearts. A little delay might put the case beyond Satanic power, hence the promptness of diabolical activity. O that we were half as quick and active in the service of our Lord; one half as quick to seize every opportunity for blessing the souls of men!

No doubt Satan acts at times directly upon the thoughts of men. He personally suggested to Judas the selling of his Master, and many another evil insinuation has he cast into men's minds. He tears away the good thoughts which would be the life of a man's soul. Insatiably malicious, he cannot endure that a single divine truth should bless the heart. Fearful blasphemies, lewd imaginations, gross unbeliefs, or vain frivolities are cast by him into the mind like infernal bombshells to destroy any new-born thought which looks toward Christ and salvation. At one time he fascinates the mind, and at another he terrifies it; his one aim being to distract the man's thoughts from the gospel.

As Satan cannot be everywhere present at one time, he frequently does his evil work by his servants, sending the inferior spirits to act as fowls in devouring the seed, and these again employ various agents. With great cunning the common incidents of life are used in the evil business. If the preacher has some unusual feature to his manner, utterance, or appearance, this becomes the 'bird' which devours the seed: the hearer is so taken up with a trifling oddity in the minister that he forgets the truth which was spoken. Should an anecdote be related, an illustration employed, or something said that awakens something in the hearer's mind, then the devil's 'bird' plucks that Word out of the heart to make room for vain thoughts.

Or, once the sermon has been preached, some event may be used by the devil to accomplish his purpose, such as a lost umbrella, congestion in the aisle, a foolish jest overheard in the crowd, or the absurd dress of some unknown person. Any such things may be used to snatch away the Word. Little does it matter whether the seed is devoured by black crows or white doves, by great fowls or little sparrows, if the Word does not abide in the heart it cannot bring forth fruit, and hence the devil arranges that somehow he will take away the seed at once.

If Satan never visits a place of worship at any other time, he will be sure to be there when revival has begun. He lets alone many a pulpit, but when an earnest man really begins preaching, Satan comes immediately.

II. Secondly, we will now for a moment notice Satan's POWER. '...and taketh away the word out of their hearts.' It is not said that he *tries* to do it, but that he *actually* does so. He sees, he comes, and he conquers. The Word is there, and the devil takes it away as easily as a bird removes a seed from the wayside. What sway the evil one has over the human mind unless a divine power is put forth with the Word. Perhaps from the striking manner in which it was stated, a little of the truth abides in the memory, but the enemy takes it quite out of the heart; and so the main part, the all-important part of our work is undone.

We may be foolish enough to aim at the head only, but he who is crafty beyond all craft deals with the heart. Whoever will may win the intellect, but if Satan can keep the affections he is quite content. To the man's heart the good seed is lost, because the fowls have devoured it. It has become to him a nullity, having no power over him, putting no life in him. Not a trace is left, any more than there would be a mark remaining of seed cast on the wayside after the birds had taken it away: so effectual is the work of the prince of the power of the air. When Satan thinks it worth his while to come, and come immediately, he means business, and he takes care that his errand shall not fail.

He is more than a match for preacher and hearer together if the Holy Spirit is not there to thwart him. He has also acquired fresh cunning by long practice in his accursed business. He knows the human heart better than anyone except its Maker. For thousands of years he has studied the anatomy of our nature, and is conversant with our weaker points. We are all young and inexperienced compared with this ancient tempter, all narrow in our views and limited in our experience compared with this serpent. Small wonder that he takes away the Word which is sown in hard hearts.

Moreover, he derives his chief power from the hearer's condition of soul. It is easy for birds to pick up seed which lies exposed on a trodden path. If the soil had been good and the seed had entered it, he would have had far greater difficulty, and might even have been foiled. But a hard heart does the devil's work for him in great measure. He need not use violence or craft, for there lies the unreceived Word upon the surface of the soul, and he simply takes it away.

The power of the evil one largely springs from our own lack of prayer. Let us pray the Lord to renew the heart that the testimony of Jesus may never be taken away. Great is the need for such prayer. Our adversary is no imaginary being, his existence is real, his presence constant, his power immense, his activity indefatigable. 'Lord, match him, and overmatch him. Drive away this foulest of fowls; break up the soil of the soul, and let thy truth truly live and graciously grow within us.'

III. Our short sermon closes, thirdly, with the devil's PURPOSE. He is a sound theologian, and knows that salvation is by believing in the Lord Jesus, and so he fears above all lest men should 'believe and be saved'. The substance of the gospel lies in those few words, 'believe and be saved,' and in proportion to Satan's hatred of that gospel, we ought to prize it. He is not so much afraid of works as of faith. If he can lead men to work, or feel, or do anything in the place of believing, he is content, but he dreads people believing, because God has coupled it with being saved. Every hearer should know this, and be instructed thereby to turn all his attention to the point which the devil considers to be worthy of his whole activity. If the destroyer labours to prevent the heart's believing, the wise will have their wits about them, and regard faith as the one thing needful.

'Lest they should believe and be saved', Satan takes away the Word out of their hearts. Here also is wisdom hidden within the enemy's cunning. If the gospel remains in contact with the heart its tendency is to produce faith. The seed abiding in the soil springs up and brings forth fruit, and so will the gospel display its living power if it dwells within the man, and therefore the devil hastens to take it away. The Word of God is the sword of the Spirit, and the devil does not like to see it lie near the sinner for fear it should wound him. He dreads the influence of truth upon the conscience, and if he cannot prevent a man's hearing it he labours to prevent his meditating upon it. 'Faith cometh by hearing, and hearing by the word of God': to obliterate that which has been heard is the Satanic method of preventing faith.

Here, again, is a practical word for the ear of prudence: let us keep the gospel as much as possible near the mind of the unconverted. Let us sow and sow again if, hopefully, some grain may take root. In planting certain seeds farmers used to put in 'one for the worm, and one for the crow, and then a third which would surely grow,' and we must do the same. In the book of *Jeremiah* the Lord describes his own action thus: 'I spake unto you, rising up early and speaking, but ye heard not; and I called you, but ye answered not.' Surely, if the Lord himself continued to speak to an unresponsive people we need not complain if much of our preaching should appear to be in vain.

There is life in the seed of the gospel, and it will grow if it can be got into the soil of the heart; let us therefore have faith in it, and never dream of obtaining a crop except by the old-fashioned way of sowing good seed. The devil evidently hates the Word, let us then keep to it, and sow it everywhere.

Reader or hearer, you have often heard the gospel, have you heard it in vain? Then the devil has had more to do with you than you have dreamed. Is the thought a pleasant one? The presence of the devil is defiling and degrading, and he has been hovering over you as the birds over the high road, and lighting upon you to steal away the Word. Think of this. You are missing fellowship with the Father and with his Son Jesus Christ by your unbelief, and instead you are having fellowship with Satan. Is not this horrible? Instead of the Holy Ghost dwelling in you as he dwells in all believers, the prince of darkness is making you his resort, coming and going at his pleasure into your mind.

You remember Jacob's dream of a ladder, and angels ascending and descending from himself to Heaven. Your life-experience may be pictured by another ladder which descends into the dark abyss, and up and down its rungs foul spirits come and go to yourself! Does not this startle you? The Lord grant it may. Do you desire a change? May the Holy Spirit turn your heart into good ground, and then shall the seed of divine grace grow in you, and produce faith in the Lord Jesus.

The Numbered People

by C. H. Spurgeon

**A short sermon written at Menton in 1879
urging members to work for the Lord.
(Edited)**

'According to the commandment of the Lord they were numbered by the hand of Moses, every one according to his service, and according to his burden: thus were they numbered of him, as the Lord commanded Moses' *(Numbers 4.49)*.

ISRAEL IN THE WILDERNESS is acknowledged in some respects to have been a type of the church in its present condition. The tribe of Levi was in a peculiar and inner sense the type of Christians who under the great High Priest are set apart for the service of the Lord and his church. To Levi the carriage of the holy vessels from place to place was committed, each family of the tribe being made responsible for the safe and reverent transport of a certain part of the sacred furniture.

Since nothing in the service of the God of order may be left to hazard but everything must be done decently and according to arrangement, all the Levites were counted, and then appointed each man to his service. Those persons who in hackneyed phrase cry out against 'system' ought to be told that the Lord has always had a system, not only in nature and providence, but also in his own courts.

There is an admirable 'economy' in the palace of the great King. Whatever degree of disorder, waste, and riot may surround other monarchs, nothing of the kind will be found beneath the shadow of the divine throne. He who counts the stars and calls them all by their names, leaves nothing unarranged in his own service. His church, therefore, should exhibit the discipline of an army, and all his warriors should know how to keep rank. Though we are not under the law, we are not without law to Christ, nor do we wish to be, for his commandments are not grievous.

At this season, when our church is making a most earnest effort to glorify the Lord by seeking conversions, we would muster all the servants of our Master and summon each one to take his appointed place and service. The work of the Lord is to be done, and should be done well, and done by us all most cheerfully and enthusiastically. Gather, therefore, yourselves together and let each redeemed one take up his burden, and bear it before the Lord in due order. Like Moses, we would call you out one by one, and give you a charge as from the Lord.

Our text contains authority for the muster-roll, appointment for the individuals, and an account of the actual execution of the command. Upon each of these an absent officer of your company would try to say a little, as the Holy Spirit may enable him.

I. Here is, first, authority for the muster-roll, 'according to the commandment of the Lord they were numbered.' The armies of Israel are not ours to lead where we like, nor even to count so that the number may be to our own honour. The counting of apostles and disciples is lawful enough, for it was frequently done in the best days of the church, but statistics may be taken in such a spirit as to be the occasion of sin. In no such manner would we now number the host unto the battle, but would summon the chosen of the Lord to the Lord's work and in the Lord's name.

Believers in Christ Jesus, you are now called forth to service, because like the tribe of Levi you are the Lord's. He views you as the church of the firstborn, as the redeemed from among men, and as his peculiar portion and inheritance, and therefore above all other men you are under his special rule and governance. The Lord said unto Moses, 'The Levites shall be mine: I am the Lord,' and he has made the same declaration concerning all those that fear the Lord and that think upon his name: 'They shall be mine, saith the Lord, in that day when I make up my jewels.'

Upon whom shall we call to perform the work of the Lord but upon those who are his own? Obligations as powerful as they are honourable are upon them. 'Ye are not your own, ye are bought with a price, therefore glorify God in your body, and in your spirit, which are God's.' Do you feel a shrinking from being numbered and called out for active service? Is not this an evil and unworthy sensation? Should you not far rather account it your glory to be called out with the dedicated ones?

Again, brethren, the Lord may well call you to this service, seeing he has given you to his Son, even as he gave the Levites to Aaron, as it is written (Numbers 3.9) – 'they are wholly given unto him out of the children of Israel.' The Lord had also said, 'Bring the tribe of Levi near, and present them before Aaron the priest, that they may minister unto him.' They were happy thus to serve the head of their own tribe, and more happy still are we to serve the Lord Christ, who is the firstborn among many brethren. Because you belong to Christ, therefore, do not hide yourselves from his service, but come forward with alacrity.

Here are a few of the claims which the Lord has upon you. Will you not own the supreme authority which calls you to active service?

II. Under our second head we shall notice the appointment of the individuals – 'every one according to his service, and according to his burden.' By our varied gifts, positions, offices, and opportunities we are as much set apart to special services as were the sons of

Kohath, Gershon, and Merari. One family bore the ark and the other the holy vessels. Another had charge of the sacred hangings, and a third carried the boards and the pillars and framework of the tabernacle. But supreme authority had set each family its own special service and burden.

So it is among us, and let us see to it that we observe the divine appointment. 'Having then gifts differing according to the grace that is given to us, whether ministry, let us wait on our ministering: or he that teacheth, on teaching; or he that exhorteth, on exhortation: he that giveth, let him do it with simplicity; he that ruleth, with diligence; he that sheweth mercy, with cheerfulness.' Great evils arise out of persons mistaking their calling, and undertaking things of which they are not capable. On the other hand the success of Christian work, in large measure, arises out of tasks being carried out by the right people.

In the march through the wilderness the sons of Merari never interfered with the burdens of the sons of Kohath, or the arrangements would have been sadly disturbed. Each one took up his allotted load and went on his way rejoicing, no one jostling his fellow. If we could bring all our workers into similar order how like an army would the church become, and how beautiful would be her battle-array. 'A place for every one and every one in his place' should be the practical motto of our congregations, and the people should be numbered, not according to worldly rank or self-estimate, but 'every one according to his service'.

It is to be noticed here that the Levites only rendered this service, 'from thirty years old and upward even unto fifty years old'. We rejoice that it is not so among us under the gospel, for there is work for the young people, and also for the aged. Little children, and young men and maidens, may take their places among the servitors of the Prince of Peace, and he who leans upon his staff for age shall not find himself dismissed from his Master's beloved service.

No women are mentioned as bearers of the tabernacle and its holy furniture. It was a work for which they were scarcely fitted, and an economy under which they were seldom employed. Here, too, we have a great change, for there is neither male nor female in Christ Jesus, and in their own way the sisters are our fellow-servants, even as they are our fellow-heirs. Never can women be forgotten in any enumeration of the forces of the church. What could we do without them?

Let it not be forgotten, then, that our Lord Jesus Christ, the great Head of the church, calls out all his redeemed to his service, and that he lays upon each one a burden which no one else can carry. It should be the joy of each believer to know what it is that his shoulders are permitted to bear, and then he should gladly take up the ennobling load. Exemption there can be none, unless a man will dare to claim that he was never bought with a price. Each one throughout life must be 'stedfast, unmoveable, always abounding in the work of the Lord.'

III. Thirdly, our text is the summary of the chapter in which we have an **account of the actual fulfilment of the Lord's command by Moses**. He numbered each family, and cast up the total of the tribe, at the same time mentioning in detail the distinctive service of each. We would imitate him at this important moment, and take the census of those who are consecrated to the Lord's own service.

Where are you, then, who can bear the heavier service of the sanctuary, carrying its pillars, and the boards, and the sockets thereof? You are now needed to speak in the meetings, to lead the people in prayer, to order the assemblies, and to take the heavier work of this holy business. The Lord Jesus should have able men to speak for him and he deserves the best of the best. Now is the hour, where is the man? Let no diffidence or love of ease keep one back who might make known the gospel and win a soul for Jesus. By the curse of Meroz when they came not to the help of the Lord against the mighty, we would charge all Christians of influence and ability to hasten to the field.

But where are you who can only carry the pins and the cords? Your burden is lighter, but probably your strength is also less, and lighter though your load may be, the matters which you carry are quite as essential as the pillars and the boards. Where are you? You who can say a few words to lonely enquiring ones; or you who can do no more than pray, where are you? At your posts, or idling? Answer, and answer quickly, for time and need are pressing. If the load which you can carry be so very small be all the more ready to bear it.

Are you a lover of the Lord Jesus and do you wish to be omitted from the roll call? If so, then you should admit it yourself, and state it plainly to your conscience. Do not pretend to be a labourer and remain a loiterer, but openly avow to your own soul that you stand all the day idle, and feel fully justified in so doing. Deny your Lord his due, but do it to his face. Tell him openly that you do not intend to spend your days in glorifying his name. Do you shrink from this honest refusal of service? You need not do so because it is not unusual, for as Nabal said, 'there be many servants now a days that break away every man from his master.'

It is plain, however, that you have no stomach for so clear a rejection of your Lord. Come, then, and take your place among those who are striving together to honour their Lord. At this time your help will be precious. Seek a new anointing, and then hasten to the work. Is not the Holy Ghost in you? Does he not prompt you to seek the salvation of others? Is not the Lord Jesus the model to which grace conforms you? How can this be if you have little or no love for the souls of your neighbours?

Your pastor calls you, though far away. By all our mutual love he beseeches you to fulfil your ministry every one according to his service and according to his burden. But, far above this, your God, your Saviour, your Comforter call you with one voice. Can you refuse the heavenly vocation?

Appendix
The First 'Suffering Letter'

Rome, 7th December 1871

To my beloved Church and friends in general

Beloved in the Lord, having felt it to be my duty to leave England for a short time to prevent a return of my former complaint, I am bound gratefully to acknowledge the good hand of the Lord upon me during my short sojourn abroad. I hope to return in a brief season, so strengthened as to continue to labour on for a considerable period without another pause. I take this opportunity of thanking my affectionate church and kind friends, for their innumerable acts of generous sympathy, in aiding our College and Orphanage, and especially for those many prayers which were turned to my comfort and healing in my late illness, and are the means of my upholding in my ever-growing service for the Lord. The Lord return into their bosoms a thousandfold the good which faithful friends have implored for me, and make me far more than ever the means of blessing them by my ministry.

Just now I implore a renewal of those prayers with increased earnestness, for a revival of religion is greatly needed; and it would be a sure evidence of its speedy coming, if believers united in prayer for it. Already the flame is kindled at the Tabernacle, but it needs to be fanned into a mighty conflagration. Our country requires a divine visitation, and the promise of it only needs to be pleaded to be fulfilled. Brethren, as one man, cry mightily to the God of our Lord Jesus Christ, the Father of glory, beseeching him to put his hand to the work, and magnify his Son in the eyes of all the people. Standing where Satan's seat is, in the midst of ten thousand idols, I beseech those who worship God in the Spirit to wrestle in prayer for times of refreshing, that all lands may know that Jesus Christ is Lord. How long shall the name of Jesus be blasphemed by the idolatries of Antichrist? It may be that the times of darkness will last till the children of light cry out bitterly, day and night, by reason of soul anguish. Then will God avenge his own elect, and that speedily.

As I have trodden the Appian Way I have rejoiced that Jesus, whom Paul preached, is yet alive, and is certain in due season to put down his enemies. Already he has desolated the Colosseum where his faithful martyrs poured forth their blood; the pagan power has fallen, and so also shall the papal, and all other which opposes his kingdom. Let us proclaim a spiritual crusade, and set up our banners by redoubled prayer. It is certain that supplication produces marvellous results in Heaven and earth; its power is proven in our own personal experience, and throughout the history of the church. Brethren, LET US PRAY.

Yours, for Jesus' sake,

C. H. Spurgeon

www.MetropolitanTabernacle.org

The Metropolitan Tabernacle is still a large congregation in central London proclaiming the gospel of salvation and the doctrines of grace.

See web site for details of services, *Sword & Trowel* magazine, Seminary, many other ministries, and free sermon downloads.

The Faith
Great Christian Truths
Peter Masters

119 pages, paperback, ISBN 978 1 870855 54 9

There is nothing like this popular, non-technical sweep through key themes of the Christian faith, highlighting very many inspiring and enlivening points. It often takes an unusual approach to a topic in order to bring out the full wonder and significance.

It is designed to be enjoyed by seasoned Christians, and also by all who want to explore the great features of the faith, and discover the life of the soul.

CONTENTS:

The Mysterious Nature of a Soul	The New Birth
What God is Actually Like	Why the Resurrection?
The Fall of Man	Prophecies of Resurrection
The Three Dark Hours of Calvary	The Holy Trinity

Faith, Doubts, Trials and Assurance
Peter Masters

139 pages, paperback, ISBN 978 1 870855 50 1

Ongoing faith is essential for answered prayer, effective service, spiritual stability and real communion with God. In this book many questions are answered about faith, such as –

How may we assess the state of our faith?
How can faith be strengthened?
How should difficult doubts be handled?
How can we tell if troubles are intended to chastise or to refine?
What can be done to obtain assurance?
Can a believer commit the unpardonable sin?
Exactly how is the Lord's presence felt?

The author provides answers, with much pastoral advice, drawing on Scripture throughout.

Heritage of Evidence

Peter Masters

127 pages, illustrated, paperback, ISBN 978 1 870855 39 6

In today's atheistic climate most people have no idea how much powerful evidence exists for the literal accuracy and authenticity of the biblical record. The British Museum holds a huge number of major discoveries that provide direct corroboration and background confirmation for an immense sweep of Bible history. This survey of Bible-authenticating exhibits has been designed as a guide for visitors, and also to give pleasure and interest to readers unable to tour the galleries. It will also be most suitable for people who need to see the accuracy and inspiration of the Bible.

The 'tour' followed here started life over forty years ago and has been used by many thousands of people including youth and student groups.

Almost every item viewed on the tour receives a full colour photograph. Room plans are provided for every gallery visited showing the precise location of artefacts, and time-charts relate the items to contemporary kings and prophets. The book is enriched by pictures and descriptions of famous 'proofs' in other museums.

Not Like Any Other Book

Peter Masters

161 pages, paperback, ISBN 978 1 870855 43 3

Faulty Bible interpretation lies at the root of every major mistake and 'ism' assailing churches today, and countless Christians are asking for the old, traditional and proven way of handling the Bible to be spelled out plainly.

A new approach to interpretation has also gripped many evangelical seminaries and Bible colleges, an approach based on the ideas of unbelieving critics, stripping the Bible of God's message, and leaving pastors impoverished in their preaching.

This book reveals what is happening, providing many brief examples of right and wrong interpretation. The author shows that the Bible includes its own rules of interpretation, and every believer should know what these are.

Physicians of Souls
The Gospel Ministry
Peter Masters

285 pages, paperback, ISBN 978 1 870855 34 1

'Compelling, convicting, persuasive preaching, revealing God's mercy and redemption to dying souls, is seldom heard today. The noblest art ever granted to our fallen human race has almost disappeared.'

Even where the free offer of the gospel is treasured in principle, regular evangelistic preaching has become a rarity, contends the author. These pages tackle the inhibitions, theological and practical, and provide powerful encouragement for physicians of souls to preach the gospel. A vital anatomy or order of conversion is supplied with advice for counselling seekers.

The author shows how passages for evangelistic persuasion may be selected and prepared. He also challenges modern church growth techniques, showing the superiority of direct proclamation. These and other key topics make up a complete guide to soul-winning.

Worship in the Melting Pot
Peter Masters

148 pages, paperback, ISBN 978 1 870855 33 4

'Worship is truly in the melting pot,' says the author. 'A new style of praise has swept into evangelical life shaking to the foundations traditional concepts and attitudes.' How should we react? Is it all just a matter of taste and age? Will churches be helped, or changed beyond recognition?

This book presents four essential principles which Jesus Christ laid down for worship, and by which every new idea must be judged.

Here also is a fascinating view of how they worshipped in Bible times, including their rules for the use of instruments, and the question is answered – What does the Bible teach about the content and order of a service of worship today?

www.wakemantrust.org